TERROR
OVER
ELIZABETH
NEW JERSEY

TERROR
OVER
ELIZABETH
NEW JERSEY

THREE PLANE CRASHES IN 58 DAYS
AND THE FIGHT FOR NEWARK AIRPORT

PETER ZABLOCKI

THE
History
PRESS

Published by The History Press
Charleston, SC
www.historypress.com

First published 2021

Manufactured in the United States

ISBN 9781467149679

.

Library of Congress Control Number: 2021945859

Notice: The information in this book is true and complete to the best of our knowledge. It is offered without guarantee on the part of the author or The History Press. The author and The History Press disclaim all liability in connection with the use of this book.

For my mom, who will be missed forever and always. And for my dad—the person who reminds me each day that no matter what, life is beautiful.

P.Z.

CONTENTS

Acknowledgements   9
Introduction   11

1. Newark Airport and the Dawn of Commercial Travel   19
2. The Ruckus Before the Storm   29
3. When Planes Started Falling   39
4. The Twentieth Plane in Two Hours   51
5. "Can't Make It Back"   63
6. A Battle for the Fate of an Airport   79
7. Back to the New Normal   87

Epilogue   95
Notes   99
About the Author   111

ACKNOWLEDGEMENTS

As always, a sincere thank-you goes out to my wife and children for putting up with me being buried in books and old newspapers and practically glued to my computer monitor and keyboard for hours and days at a time. I would also like to acknowledge my past mentors: Muhammad Awais, Peter Pra, Ed Frankosky and Scott Gambale. It is because of the hindsight of these individuals back then that today I can call myself a writer. Mr. Awais, thank you for awakening in me the love for reading. Pete, thank you for teaching me the value of hard work. Ed, thank you for helping me learn from youthful mistakes. And Scott, thank you for opening my mind to challenging my assumptions and seeing history in a different way.

A sincere thank-you also goes to Newark Public Library's Beth F. Cummings and Greg Guderian for granting me access to the various files associated with the Elizabeth plane crashes and sparking my interest in expanding my research and creating the work that you hold in your hands. This work would not be possible without them.

INTRODUCTION

January 22, 1952

Henrietta Reid was thirty years old, a blonde considered pretty and full of life. She was a mother of two, with another baby on the way. She caught herself gently holding on to her already bulging stomach, as she had often done for the past few weeks. She continued wiping down plates as she took them out of the cabinet to prepare them for the family birthday party honoring her mother, who was turning forty-nine. Henrietta was hosting. Their apartment on Broadway Street in Elizabeth was small, but it was more than enough for their growing family.

The great noise was almost instantaneously followed by loud sirens and fire engines racing down past her home. She did not know how long she stood there after the plate fell out of her hand and crashed to the floor. She was suspended in time. "I had a premonition," she later said, "[I walked into the living room and] I turned on the radio. Then I heard the bulletin. And I knew that Tom's plane was due to go over about that time."[1]

Tom had been a pilot during World War II and began flying for American Airlines shortly afterward. The young couple got married as soon as the great conflict ended in 1945 and had just recently saved enough money to build their forever home in Point Pleasant, New Jersey. It was nearly finished. Just a few more flights, a little bit more money and a little bit more time. Henrietta picked up the phone and called American Airlines. The company would not tell her if it was her husband's plane that was

Mrs. Henrietta Reid, widow of American Airlines pilot Thomas J. Reid, who died when his plane crashed in a residential section of Elizabeth four blocks away from their home in January 1952. *From* The Record *(Hackensack). January 24, 1952.*

involved. The person promised to call her right back. She picked up her one-year-old daughter, Robin, and sat on the floor next to the three-year-old, Eileen, who was playing with her toys. The young wife sat there, staring blankly. She wanted to cry but could not even draw in enough breath to do so. "It seemed forever before they called back," she said, "And then they told me...it was Tom's plane that crashed."[2] She placed her hand on her stomach and knew their unborn child would never know his father.

Three blocks away, disaster units rushed to the scene. The young men had been through this before. Just a month prior, they were clearing the debris from another airplane crash on the other side of town in Elizabeth. The rain was picking up. It seemed like the floodwaters had opened above them, as if the sky itself was weeping. Yet the men worked, their feet buried in ankle-deep mud, their eyes blinded by the floodlights set up around them. Despite the weather, a crowd of more than four thousand people gathered behind the police barriers.[3] Some of those who called Elizabeth their home for many years could not believe this was happening again. Their tears mixed with the rain. They watched mangled bodies being lifted gently from the rubble and splintered wood and shattered plane metal. This time, the plane had crashed into even more buildings. One of the young workers on the scene looked up at a woman sobbing uncontrollably. "My baby is in there."[4] He looked down. He did not want her to see his tears. Perhaps she would not; it was dark and wet. He then noticed a book among the debris, right by his foot. He bent down and picked it up. Turning it into the floodlight and wiping the mud off it, he first noticed the title, *Passport into Peril*.[5] He no longer cared who saw him crying.

In less than three weeks, he would be there again, this time pulling bodies out of yet another wreck, of yet another plane crash. By that time, Elizabeth's mayor, James Kirk, had already begun referring to his city as one existing beneath "an umbrella of death."[6]

IT WOULD BE POINTLESS to hide the fact that when we think of a plane crash today, it evokes the moving pictures of planes flying into the World Trade Center on September 11, 2001. It was, is and hopefully will remain the most important air disaster in American history. Yet it would be equally foolish to think that it was the only one to elicit such an emotional response. All airplane crashes are tragedies in their own ways. But what if there are two in the same place within mere weeks of each other? A calamity? A misfortune? What if there are *three* in the same city, all within a span of just fifty-eight days? Certainly, one is left scratching his head. No, it cannot be. Yet, that is exactly what transpired in Elizabeth, New Jersey, in the early 1950s. What really happened in those months between December 1951 and February 1952? Why did it happen? Perhaps most importantly, what did we learn from it? After all these years, why is it that we still cannot look away?

"Plane crashes are terrifying," wrote journalist Mark Hay. "As humans, they play to some sort of visceral fear inside us—we aren't supposed to fly, so the thought of something going wrong up there is particularly unsettling."[7] The first plane to crash in Elizabeth did so exactly forty-eight years and a day after the Wright brothers first conquered the heavens in their flimsy, homemade wooden aircraft on December 17, 1903, in Kitty Hawk, North Carolina. In nearly half a century, Wilbur and Orville's dream had evolved into jet-powered aircraft, helicopters and even rocket technology–enabled experimental spacecraft. By 1919, the airplane had proved itself an indispensable war weapon. It was also the year when the first plane crossed the Atlantic Ocean. Of course, who can forget Charles Lindbergh's first nonstop transatlantic solo flight, in the *Spirit of St. Louis*, from New York to Paris, France—barely eight years later. It did not take long after that for companies to see the potential of an airplane as a major means of transportation. By 1926, Congress had adopted the Air Commerce Act, which authorized the secretary of commerce to designate air routes, develop air navigation systems and license pilots and aircraft.[8] Commercial flight was finally a reality.

The aircraft industry evolved with blazing speed, quickly surpassing the rail system as the preferred means of travel and ushering in the so-called Golden Age of Travel of the 1950s. Americans were obsessed with the idea of flight, something that just a few short decades earlier was nothing short of a science fiction notion taken out of an Edgar Rice Burroughs *Mars* novel. Aircraft companies scrambled to satisfy people's curiosity. And technological developments in aviation managed to keep pace with people's escalating interests. By 1929, only some twenty-odd years after the Wrights' wooden bicycle with wings took its first flight, Pan American Airways inaugurated its first passenger flight from Miami to San Juan.[9] This was quickly followed five years later by the first Boeing-designed commercial aircraft with a pressurized cabin. The American masses' travel habits were altered forever. By the conclusion of World War II and through the "Fabulous Fifties," airline travel had made the world seem smaller, but for an average person it was the glamorous experience that was the most alluring part. Delta Air Lines, American Airlines and Pan Am Airways became the glamour companies that received the red-carpet treatment, proclaimed a *Newsweek* article from 1958. Newly constructed and enlarged existing airports were lavished with subsidies and tax breaks as long-distance flights whisked Americans to faraway playgrounds and vice versa.[10] Both the Atlantic and the Pacific Oceans became manageable, essentially putting out to pasture the long-standing standard of passenger liners. While flying was relatively expensive at first, by the end of the decade, millions of Americans were visiting Europe and Asia via air travel.

Due to cost reductions in the 1950s, the number of passengers traveling annually was multiplying. In 1929, the cost per passenger mile was twelve cents as compared to five cents in 1939. The number of people traveling jumped from 2.5 million in 1937 to 45 million in 1952 (the year of the Newark Airport/Elizabeth crashes) and 90 million by 1957.[11] When studying the events that transpired in New Jersey in the winter of 1951 and 1952, one cannot ignore the sheer fact that as popular as air travel was at the time, it was still in its relative infancy. In fact, it was only fifty years removed from the Wright brothers' flying contraption. The idea of trying to squeeze immense airports, with their massive airfields accommodating large planes, as close to potential customers in suburbs and heavy metropolitan areas as possible did not yet consider the context of safety. In fact, it was thought, the closer the airfield to city congestion the better. After Lindbergh's famous flight, President Herbert Hoover's air commission drew plans for a major airport in the meadowlands of Newark, New Jersey. The choice was carefully but also geographically and strategically calculated, as the proposed airfield would be not only within the city limits of Newark, one of the largest commercial centers of the state, but also a short fifteen-mile hike from New York City. Newspapers from the 1920s boasted of a highway system connecting the two. "A speed of 40 miles per hour is permitted, which will not be impeded by any cross traffic. Upon its completion, the airport will be 12 minutes by automobile from Canal Street and Broadway, New York."[12] As the city itself did not have enough room to hold any additional airstrips in New York City proper, Newark became the ideal solution.

Government safety regulations and oversight of commercial air traffic were still in their early years. And although in place since the mid-1920s, they were still evolving thirty years later. Concurrently, air travel was hampered by the evolving plane technology, with most of the pilots being World War II carryovers without proper commercial flight training in urban and suburban environments, to add to the already mentioned infant air control regulations. In 1951, when the first crash took place in Elizabeth, the Civil Aeronautics Administration (CAA)—concerned with air-traffic control, safety programs and overall airway development—was barely a decade old. With the airplanes themselves becoming outdated and their technology not yet fully reliable—at least until the jet age in the latter part of the decade—the 1950s witnessed many crashes, prompting the creation of another agency, the Civil Aeronautics Board (CAB). The organization's job was to investigate airplane accidents but also, perhaps more importantly, establish safety regulations based on lessons learned from them. It was not a coincidence that the crashes in Elizabeth all involved outdated airplane technology. The first crash in New Jersey during that fateful winter was a twin-engine, repurposed military plane nicknamed the "Flying Coffin" because of its wartime record; the second was a short-lived Convair CV-240, which ceased production in 1954 after only seven years and was at the center of seventeen crashes between 1952 and 1960; the third was a Douglas DC-3, whose civil production ended prior to the U.S. entrance into World War II. And while the CAB was not always able to find specific flaws with the airplanes in all three instances that might have caused the unfortunate events that transpired, the facts of outdated and unreliable technology need not be forgotten.

In that sense, the horrible trilogy that transpired in Elizabeth was the product of a growing industry that had not yet hit its stride. But is that it? Can it be that simple? Although airplane accidents could hardly ever be attributed to just one factor—with the element of human error never discarded out of the equation—the chain of events of December, January and February 1951–52 has never occurred since. So, what changed? Even at the time, in one of the first books of its kind, *Plane Crash: The Mysteries of Major Air Disasters and How They Were Solved* (published in 1958), scholar Clayton Knight placed the three crashes in the "Some Strange Accidents" section of his book.[13] However, this did not take away from the fact that they did happen. The book you hold in your hands explores the events leading

Newark Airport, as seen from the Newark Meadows. Picture taken circa 1946. *Courtesy of Newark Public Library.*

up to the crashes. It re-creates the tragedies using firsthand accounts from those who witnessed them—or perhaps, for lack of a better word, survived them. It uncovers their aftermath—a fight and struggle of a city's people to feel safe in their own homes. Finally, it explores the lessons that should have been learned before the crashes ever occurred and just might have been after they already did. The work draws heavily on newspapers of the time, as well as various books and studies on the history of aviation, air disasters and the histories of the cities of Newark and Elizabeth. It also relies on firsthand accounts from the time and recollections since. While no other historical book has been written about the topic, the closest one could get to read about the events described here is in Judy Blume's 2015 novel *In the Unlikely Event.* The chart-topping author is herself an eyewitness to the events, as she was a teenager living in Elizabeth when the crashes took place. Her extensive research into the event, and the amazing novel that followed, is perhaps one of the biggest inspirations for this work.

Why do people care so much about plane crashes? According to Eric Wilson, a professor at Wake Forest University and the author of the 2012's *Everyone Loves a Good Train Wreck: Why We Can't Look Away*, it has a lot to do with our general obsession with disasters, which stems from both voyeuristic and empathetic impulses.[14] As stated in his book, fixating on disaster reports oftentimes brings out the best in us, as they evoke feelings of empathy for those suffering as well as a desire for a deeper understanding of the meanings of suffering and death as a whole. "I also think that we probably get a feeling of relief when watching disaster coverage, relief that this terrible thing didn't happen to us," Wilson added.[15] The scale and cinematic images that accompany these disasters make them that much harder to look away from. "These crashes, unlike car crashes, usually kill hundreds of people all at once.…[Also] we can imagine ourselves in such a crash—if it could happen to them, then it could happen to us. Most of us can't imagine ourselves dying in a war in the same way since most of us have never fought in a war."[16] Last but not least, as is the case with most air disasters, the Elizabeth trilogy included, there is the element of mystery. It often takes a while for the probes and investigations to be concluded, making the events stay in the news for prolonged periods of time.

As there have not been any more commercial plane crashes in Elizabeth from nearby Newark Airport since 1952, the events of that winter have disappeared from the news—a blessing and a testament to improved aero technology, safety measures and pilot training. By 2014, the global jet accident rate was 0.23 percent, the equivalent of one accident for every 4.4 million flights. All this while carrying a record 3.3 billion passengers in that year. At the time of the Elizabeth crashes—when airlines carried fewer than 140 million passengers—there were eighty-seven crashes, killing 1,597 people.[17] Because there have not been any more such disasters in the area that would evoke the memories of those harrowing fifty-eight days, newspapers have not had the need to dig them out to compare them to anything resembling them since. Still, in 2018, Chuck O'Donnell of *Union News Daily* sought out and interviewed the survivors of the January 1952 crash. Many of those who shared their experiences freely proclaimed that if it were not for pure chance, they would not be alive today to tell their stories. Eugene Sullivan, a retired Elizabeth firefighter who as a young child was inside a candy store in the building that was hit by the falling plane, recalled, "I'm a believer of second chances…you picture if that plane crashed, say, two seconds earlier? It would have hit right here [he points to a black-and-white photograph from after the crash, referring to the ground floor of the building], and I wouldn't be here talking to you. By all rights, I shouldn't be here talking to you."[18]

If nothing else, the harrowing events from the winter of 1951–52 need to be examined in honor of those who lost their lives, those who survived and those who continue to learn from them. This story has many heroic events that need to be highlighted and celebrated, even in tragedy. There's the pilot of the second crash, living just a few blocks away from his date with destiny, turning the plane in the last second to avoid hitting the Battin High School. There's the children from a local orphanage racing to rescue the survivors from the third crash, spread out all around them. These people, all who just survived World War II and were now living through the Korean Conflict, were fighting against the powers that be to keep their children safe.

As people walk the streets of Elizabeth, New Jersey, the signs of carnage are gone, left to the memories of those who were there. Seventy years have passed since those events, and many who were there to witness them have already gone from this world or are in the later stages of their lives. The city of Elizabeth still exists beneath the flight patterns of the nearby Newark Airport, and the Elizabeth River (into which the first flight crashed) continues to flow. The intersection of South and Wilmington Streets, the scene of the second crash, is now an ice cream shop. Kids stand outside, happily eating their soft serve vanilla ice cream, ignorant of the significance of the very site where they stand. The Dr. Orlando Edreira Academy No. 26 public school has replaced the Janet Memorial School for Orphans, where the third plane came to a halt in the playground behind the dormitory.[19] Yet these harrowing events did happen. They should not be lost to history. Here is the story of what Knight called the most devastating as well as most extraordinary tragedy in the history of air crashes. Unfortunately, it is a story that has three parts.

Chapter 1

NEWARK AIRPORT AND THE DAWN OF COMMERCIAL TRAVEL

The relationship between the city of Elizabeth, Newark Airport, and the rise in popularity of air travel began many years before the events depicted in this work. Elizabeth, New Jersey, the largest city and the county seat of Union County, was often overshadowed by its northern neighbor, Newark. The city of Newark, the most populous city in the Garden State and the county seat of Essex County, already rich in industry and shipping, only saw its claim as a major air shipping and rail hub of the tri-state area further boosted by the Second World War. In just one example, the Federal Shipyard at Port Newark was called the "Insomniac Shipyard" during the war years because it was busy twenty-four hours a day, seven days a week, turning out destroyer escorts and employing twenty thousand people in just 1943 alone.[20] Apart from their industrial and commercial backgrounds, their roles as the quasi-capitals of their respective counties, and their proximity to New York City (of which Newark was deemed closer), by the 1930s, the two cities could claim yet another connection. When examining current maps of the state, it becomes evident that the rivaling giants are connected by the Newark Airport complex. In fact, parts of the vast complex are located within both cities' borders—albeit mostly in Newark. When Newark's Mayor Thomas L. Raymond reportedly became overwhelmed with the thought of an airport, during his morning shave and after Lindbergh's transatlantic feat in 1927, he could not have foreseen the implications that his premonition would have on the area and its people a quarter of a century later. And so, the construction of the first major airport in the New York metropolitan area began in earnest, sealing its fate with the city of Elizabeth and setting in motion events that would change both forever.

IT WAS DECEMBER 6, 1919, and pilot Walter H. Stevens was battling through a heavy snowstorm from the nation's capital to land roughly seven hundred pounds of mail at Newark's Heller Field. He had done this route many times and knew the difficulties that still lay ahead. Apart from the weather—which in an open-top, early wooden airplane made the trip more of a struggle against potentially losing his fingers and toes to frostbite—there was still the Heller Field obstacle course. Newark's first airstrip was a far cry from what it would become by the twenty-first century. During the Great War, which showcased the airplane's advantages abroad, the industrial area of Essex County wanted to get into the airplane age and specifically take advantage of the new quick and efficient Federal Air Mail Service delivery system. However, the end result became a testament to what happens when idealism crashes into realism. While local business leaders sought to raise $25,000 in public subscriptions to build an airport, they managed barely one-third of the desired amount.[21] As such, Heller Field—named after a wealthy Newark real estate and business mogul—was nothing more than a crude cinder-covered runway on the edge of a golf club.

Stevens descended his plane, took a deep breath and got ready for landing at the infamous airport. In the next five minutes, which felt like ages, the pilot dodged trees, buildings, railroad tracks and telegraph wires until he finally settled his aircraft on the frozen cinder path.[22] When he looked around and sighed, he did not yet know that he had just become one of the last pilots to land there. After having read reports and examined the state of the airport firsthand, the federal government decided to withdraw the mail service in early 1920. It reasoned that it was too close to the congested areas of Newark and Elizabeth. Essentially, the decision—ironic in light of the events of 1951–52—sealed the fate of Newark's early attempt at establishing a full-fledged airport.

By the mid-1920s, Newark's commissioners were eyeing the meadowlands on the outskirts of the city as having perfect industrial potential in further solidifying the area's reputation as a major industrial hub of the tri-state area—New York, New Jersey and Connecticut. Things started to look up for the proponents of an airport when work advanced on the nearby Holland Tunnel, which would make the potential airfields in the same meadows just minutes away from the hub of New York City. Charles Lindbergh's transatlantic flight only further convinced Newark's mayor that perhaps taking advantage of the prime real estate that New York proper lacked but the nearby meadowlands provided was an even shorter route to raising Newark's status as one of the more prominent cities in the nation. Time, and not necessarily safety or future planning, was of the essence, especially if they were going to beat New York City in establishing the first major airport in the area.

At the time of Newark Airport's construction, the Big Apple lacked any municipal airports. Floyd Bennett Field, in the southern part of Brooklyn, became its first municipal airport when it opened on May 23, 1931, a few years after Newark was fully operational. Unlike its Garden State counterpart, its great distance from Manhattan made it impractical for airline service or airmail contracts.[23] It was not until the beginning of World War II in 1939, with the opening of LaGuardia Airport on North Beach in Queens, that Newark's airport was given a proper challenger for the title of New York City's primary metropolitan area airport. Unfortunately, this eagerness to be the first ultimately led to the site also becoming the area's first outdated airport. By May 31, 1940, the Civil Aeronautical Corporation (CAA) had declared the airport unsafe, and the airlines moved all operations to newer airfields at LaGuardia. Safety issues once again seemed to be the Achilles' heel for the location of the much-desired airfield. Ironically, once the airport was given the green light to operate—after it was requisitioned by the U.S. military in 1940 for the duration of the war—some of the CAA recommendations from that initial report were not addressed. Presumably, they were lost amid the many positive changes instituted during the military's tenure.

The race to build the airport was impressive even by today's standards. Still, perhaps foreshadowing the early difficulties that lasted until after the accidents of 1951–52, it was not all smooth sailing for the new endeavor. When the City of Newark first approached the newly created Port Authority of New York about the construction of an airport, the port authority set out to survey ten potential sites for just such a project in the tri-state area. Newark was placed last on its list. After all, the commission argued, the area was still very much marshland and was surrounded by major metropolitan areas, which might cause a problem with safe flight patterns. The report was followed by a push from the secretary of the federal government's Commerce for Aeronautics Committee, which—as per President Hoover's sanctioned report—concluded that the need for an airport in New York outweighed the potential cost, literal and figurative. The same report stated that Newark was best able to handle air traffic from the South and West.[24] Still, while this pressed the project past sheer planning stages and into full-blown construction, the earlier report by the more local port authority was still weighing on the minds of many members of the city commission. While it voted $5.5 million for the airport, the members discreetly and with caution declared that if the airport failed, the newly reinforced site would not be a fiscal waste, as it would still be excellent for industrial use.[25] In hindsight, it is ironic that the people who ensured the creation of an airport squeezed between the cities of Elizabeth and Newark had already foreseen its potential failure.

Work began in January 1928. Because the city was deepening a ship channel through Newark Bay, the material was abundant. Trucks hauled the scoured material three miles to the airport site, day and night. The culmination was a spread of a small mountain of 1.5 million cubic yards of wet fill, more than ten feet in height, on what would eventually become a track. Dry dirt, seven thousand discarded Christmas trees, and two hundred bank safes donated by a junk dealer were used to fill the marshlands and make the site suitable to hold the proposed airport.[26] By midsummer, 68 acres of land had been developed, with another 180 held in reserve. Soon, the airport could boast of having a 1,600-foot asphalt-treated cinder strip runaway—the first hard-surfaced commercial landing site in the United States.[27] The federal government's intentions for creating the airport became clear right away as it designated Newark Airport as the eastern airmail terminal within weeks of the construction coming to a close. It was October 1928.

Newark Airport was a massive success. Commercial flights began in 1929, with more than 4,000 planes taking off on passenger routes. Christened in 1931 as the busiest airport in the world, Newark had 120 scheduled flights daily from 5:00 a.m. until 10:00 p.m., with more than 2 million pounds of airmail also clearing the airport that year.[28] The airport could also claim to be the only one of its kind in the whole country to serve three transcontinental airlines. By mid-decade, the remainder of the marshes had been filled to accommodate the growing complex. A new 2,000-foot cross runway had been built, and the main runway running northeast–southwest (toward Elizabeth) was extended to 3,100 feet.[29] Unfortunately, as the Great Depression set in, the airport could not escape the fate of many industries of the decade. With the height of the economic malaise and airlines operating in the red, the initial policy of letting individual company leases construct their own hangars and upkeep proved to be the airport's undoing. Slowly degrading and feverishly becoming more dangerous with the ever-growing air traffic and no real updates—apart from an airport administration building built in 1935—Newark Airport was hit hard when the original ten-year airline leases expired in 1938. The city, knowing that the airport was in need of maintenance and upkeep repairs, went into negotiations with the four major airline companies—American Airlines, TWA, United Airlines and Eastern Air. The goal was to recoup some of the money needed and lost due to the diminishing demand for air travel during the Great Depression. With the companies themselves strapped for funds, they considered the airport's desire to raise the rates of their new leases as offensive. Throughout the failed negotiations, airline leases turned into month-to-month base rentals, further adding to the uncertainty of the airport's future. With taxpayer subsidies to the airport exceeding $200,000 per year, Newark mayor Meyer C. Ellenstein called on the airlines to pay $135,000, of which they would only agree to half.[30] It was 1939—less than a year from the airport first closing its doors.

It could be said that Newark Airport grew too soon, too fast and too bullish for its own good. In the end, it was the competition with the new LaGuardia Airport in New York City proper that sped up its demise. According to at least one reporter from the *Central New Jersey Home News*, writing in 1940, Mayor Fiorello La Guardia's new, "more ornate…more modern [and] larger airport," built with federal government subsidies, had lured all the aviation lines over to New York.[31] It should also be noted that the namesake mayor was able to use his influence in Washington to split up the mail contracts held by Newark with his LaGuardia fields. In the whole ordeal, one can almost overlook the real issue at play, namely that Newark Airport was busting at the seams and needed funding to keep up with the demand and wear and tear on its airfields. Mayor Ellenstein, in a newspaper interview shortly before the airport closed its hangar doors, stated that "to make the field betterments asked by the lines and the CAA [as to make the airport safer] would cost [upward of] $210,000."[32] This was money he simply did not have. It was a no-brainer for the airlines; no longer strapped with long lease contracts, they left for a more modern airfield at New York City. When the City of Newark announced that it could not operate the airport's control tower after May 31, 1940, "unless the commercial carriers paid for the facilities…as they [had] in the past," the CAA made the final call. The field had simply become too hazardous. The Civil Aeronautical Corporation stated in its report that "if the operation of the control tower were abandoned and if immediate steps were not taken to improve the runways," the field would be closed to commercial traffic.

Assistant Field Supervisor Joseph Wolf looked out onto the dark field as a big sixteen-passenger TWA airliner heading for Los Angeles soared above the Newark Airport runway at 11:54 p.m. on May 30, 1940. The airfield's glory days as one of the busiest airports in the world had come to an end. All landings and departures for the metropolitan area were moved to LaGuardia Airport, which coincidently, that same day announced a new single-day flight record with 359 planes either taking off or landing there.[33] "It's a shame to see it go. Maybe things will straighten themselves out. You never can tell," said Wolf.[34] When the traffic control tower shut down that day, Newark Airport became just a lonely, mud-spotted field—a landing site for a few charter planes, an oil company and the National Guard.[35] Within days, it was officially closed.

For a while, before its doors closed, Newark Airport's unprecedented air traffic and rapid rise to prominence brought up important safety concerns. These become relevant when examining the 1951–52 tragedies. Arrangements to avoid collisions were initially very primitive, beginning with a controller waving red and green flags while positioned at a highly visible point on the airfield to let planes know if it was safe to land. The flags were eventually replaced by flare guns, but it was not until the early 1930s that Cleveland Municipal Airport built the first air-traffic control tower, and Newark quickly followed. The pilots of approaching aircraft radioed information on their respective positions to their airline representatives at the airports, where the controllers used this information to update a map showing where all the aircraft in the vicinity were positioned and radioed pilots if there seemed any risk of a collision.[36] Yet the traffic, especially at Newark, was getting heavier. Since there was no real control of an aircraft until it was on approach to the airfield, "a number of airplanes would arrive, at similar altitude in zero visibility, joisting for a chance to land as overburdened controllers strove to avert a catastrophe."[37] The result was a traffic jam of sorts, except in the skies above the city of Newark and the nearby Elizabeth. Once the federal government regulated air-traffic control, it allowed controllers on the ground to coordinate the planes along various checkpoints on their routes and maps via radio, thus ensuring that they would not arrive near a single airstrip at the same time. Still, the system was in its early stages, and pilots did not necessarily accept these new disciplines with much happiness, sometimes leading to mixed results. To put it bluntly, modernization was an issue at Newark Airport, especially in terms of attitudes toward flying safety regulations, equipment and proper airfield maintenance.

Passengers exiting the rear of an American Airlines plane on the tarmac at Newark Airport. Late 1940s. *Courtesy of Newark Public Library.*

In 1934, Newark Airport had its first crash occur that would be attributed to the field's inadequate safety measures, especially when it came to its performance in inclement weather. A TWA mail airplane hurtled into the administration building without any reported casualties. The accident led to the airport manager installing a fence to keep the passengers away from the taxiing aircraft, but it did little to prevent another airplane from crashing in the same spot at a later date. That accident was also not fatal. With the lighting system leaving a lot to be desired, the once state-of-the-art 1929 illumination equipment did not always do its job when it came to heavy fog near Newark Airport. There are numerous reports from the late 1930s of planes having to be redirected to other airfields. Shortly before Newark's closing in 1940, an American Airlines plane was not so lucky as it dropped out of heavy fog and rain and found itself having overshot the runway. The small aircraft crash-landed one mile away in the Jersey marshlands. The five passengers, three crew and 750 pounds of mail survived without a scratch, yet the incident did attract CAA's attention.[38] After all, had it veered off slightly to the west, it would have wound up in the busy center of Elizabeth. Undoubtedly, airplane travel was still an evolving commodity and industry in the early 1930s. As one might say, kinks still had to be worked out—a dangerous proposition when human lives were at stake.

By 1946, when the City of Newark had resumed control of the airport from the U.S. Department of War, it was obvious that the military had fixed most of the glaring issues that predated the airport's takeover in 1942—although not all of them. Three four-thousand-foot-long runways were built in 1942, as was a new sixty-five-foot-high control tower. Also, an advanced lighting system was installed on both runways and approaches, the first radar installation was introduced and so many buildings were constructed that a numbering system needed to be utilized.[39] Commercial airlines were quick to return, and by October 1946, when American Airlines transferred 27 flights from LaGuardia Airport, Newark's schedule of daily flights rose to 157. While the new activity was apparent right away, the runways used by the military during the war were not adequate for such heavy commercial traffic. In fact, they needed millions of dollars to become suitable for the new demands placed on them. Newark was once again pressed for modifications. This glaring need to bring the airport up to par with modern commercial standards pushed the City of Newark to consider a lease offer that would see the Port Authority of New York take full control of the airfield complex. In 1946, the authority offered to spend $50 million on the airport and $26 million on the Newark seaport in return for a long-term lease that would give the City of Newark $100,000 a year in lieu of taxes.[40] Concurrently, it announced its intention to increase air traffic to 1,000 flights per day. Even with many locals from the nearby neighborhoods openly questioning the large expansion proposals, the official transfer of control of the airport and seaport from the city to the port authority took place in March 1948.

"Newark Airport to Be Larger by Two Thirds: Port Authority of N.Y. to Spend $1,200,000 on Expansion Program," proclaimed Passaic's *Herald News* on September 9, 1949.[41] It seemed that the often-troubled airport would finally see its due. Not surprisingly—even considering the military improvements from wartime—the airport was found inadequate and unsafe for the traffic numbers that it was seeing by early 1950. The airport area was expanded from 1,400 to 2,300 acres, roughly four times the size of LaGuardia Airport, which was incidentally also under the port authority's control. All three former runways were found unsuitable; the authority abandoned two and rehabilitated the third. In May 1950, it started work on a $9 million north–south instrument runway with the latest in safety features.[42] Perhaps most importantly, the port authority saw the creation of this new main runway as a means to fix the airport's most glaring safety problem: namely, the new instrument runway would head in a direction that would divert airplane traffic over the waters of Newark Bay and away from congested, populated areas such as nearby Elizabeth—now directly in the path of airplanes landing and taking off from the airport's main runway. Specifically, the most used field was a short distance north of the crowded built-up section of Elizabeth, between Route 1 and the New Jersey Turnpike, close to Newark Bay and the desolate widespread salt marshes.[43] According to Clayton Knight's 1958's study of air disasters, the much-used field was carelessly laid out directly across the heart of the city of Elizabeth. "Although the possibility of the occurrence of just such crashes near Newark Airport [that happened in Elizabeth] could have been foreseen [through the entirety of the airfield's existence up to that point] and was fairly widely understood to be a latent danger," he stated, "corrections had not been expedited because of those factors that so often delay the elimination of latent dangers: crashes had not occurred."[44]

To the citizens of Elizabeth and Newark's Ironbound and Weequahic sections, when it came to knowing that something was not quite right with Newark Airport, there was no need for statistical data, technical language or flight patterns. They heard it each time a plane took off with its engines revving at top speed. They felt it each time a plane passed overhead and shook their homes. And they saw it each time descending planes would nearly scrape the tops of nearby buildings. They did not need Newark commissioner Meyer Ellenstein pointing out that the airport's location was "too close to the city on the basis of accepted location standards."[45] They knew it. It would perhaps be fitting to say that the years leading up to the tragedies of the winter of 1951–52 were the calm before the storm. In this case, though, for the people of Elizabeth, New Jersey, those words would not sound quite right.

Chapter 2

THE RUCKUS BEFORE THE STORM

Some say that statistics do not lie. Once taken over by the Port Authority of New York, the Newark Airport traffic rose rapidly. By 1951, the year of the first crash, the airfield saw 100,000 plane departures and landings, with 1,355,000 passengers using Newark Airport and 104 million pounds of freight cargo being lifted off its runways. The residents of Elizabeth and the Weequahic and Ironbound sections of Newark felt nothing short of being harassed by the massive planes flying over their heads each day. The summer before the first crash witnessed more than 300 planes using the airfield each day, making the noise and vibration levels unbearable. The residents began calling it "aeronautical insomnia" and complained to the city commissions of both cities.[46] Calls for canceling the port authority lease became louder by the day, as did individual complaints in newspapers and in letters being sent to local government representatives. The fight even made it all the way to the desk of the New Jersey governor, Alfred E. Driscoll. By that time, the conversation had shifted from a mere request to have plane noise and low flights curtailed to calling for the complete relocation of the airport. Unfortunately for the citizens of cities affected by the nearby airfields, the Civil Aeronautics Administration did not share their concerns about the established flight routes and dangers of low flights out of Newark. By January 1951, at least one person, Newark commissioner Meyer C. Ellenstein, a staunch supporter of moving the airfield altogether, could easily have said "I told you so." By then, it would be too late.

For the residents of Elizabeth and the various sections of Newark, the danger seemed all too real. The endless machines flying over people's homes resulted in many sleepless nights caused by the noise and vibration that seemed to pierce the buildings below. This only added to the general feeling of unease and agitation of living near one of the biggest airports in the nation. "The roar of huge transports at all hours of the day and night [not only] disturbs the sleep of people in the…city [but also] prevents the ordinary enjoyment of their homes," stated a concerned citizen.[47] One's home, where people should feel the safest, became unbearable for many. Scared children ran out of their rooms in the middle of the night crying, as their parents' favorite TV shows' reception flickered on the screens and sometimes disappeared altogether with each passing aircraft. A simple phone conversation to seek sympathy from friends could become "unintelligible by the noise of airplanes flying so low that the faces of passengers could be seen from the ground."[48] Editorials began appearing in newspapers detailing the possibilities of reducing airplane noise. They were followed by unkept promises from the airport complex to deal with the noise and air congestion. An article in *The Record* from June 25, 1948, reassured the concerned people that scientists at Washington's National Advisory Committee for Aeronautics were working on the problem and believed that it could be solved. "The noise of an average automobile was at first great," stated the article, adding, "before experimentation and improvement in engineering techniques and the enforced use of a muffler, most automobiles sounded like a rapid discharge of a machinegun."[49] The author pointed out that the Federal Aeronautic Committee theorized that with a little more ingenuity, the noise of planes leaving airports could also be reduced to the noise level of the average automobile. When it added that the committee had already succeeded in sealing and soundproofing airplane cabins "so that the passengers hear nothing but a relaxing hum," at least one editorial shot back with the suggestion that perhaps they should spend more time worrying about the people affected on the ground instead of creating a comforting atmosphere for those in the cabins.

When challenged about the low-flying fear magnets, a spokesman for the Civil Aeronautics Administration—the chief federal organization responsible for air-traffic control, safety and airway development—admitted that that at least some of the complaints were valid. Speaking to the local paper in 1951, he pointed out that poor weather forced pilots to fly lower, sometimes as low as seven hundred, four hundred and even three hundred feet over Elizabeth and Newark's Weequahic neighborhoods. When pressed further, the administrator pointed out that no accident had occurred because of these actions and reassuringly stated, "People living near the airport have nothing to fear from the safety angle."[50] As for the noise, "people are leaving their windows open in the summer, and this makes the noise seem louder." One could see how such comments did little to quell the fears and concerns of the local citizens. In fact, they led to more statements and complaints appearing in local papers, demanding changes and even the complete removal of the airfield. "Noise Complaints Up!" called out an article from the front page of the local paper, pointing out the continued failure of Newark Airport to properly address locals' concerns.[51] Unfortunately, to many, the answers they received from the airport, their local government, the Port Authority of New York and even the CAA seemed more like excuses, halfway measures and sometimes complete ignorance.

Manager Archie M. Armstrong announced in August 1946 that the airport asked airlines to adopt a five-point program for the elimination of noise and danger caused by low-flying planes over congested areas in the vicinity of the field. He was overturned by the CAA. Instead, the federal organization gave the airport and its airlines a clean bill of health and compliance without having to make the proposed changes. The program called for an increased

A worker inspects a fuselage of a Northeast Airlines plane at Newark Airport. This was typical procedure before each flight. *Courtesy of Newark Public Library.*

rate of climb by planes leaving the field and designated that turns to be taken upon flying off from each runway; while good ideas, these were deemed unnecessary by the airlines and the CAA.[52] What was important was that, if approved, the program would have enabled aircraft to avoid residential and skyscraper areas and would concentrate most of the climbing period over Newark Bay and unpopulated districts. It at least showed that the people's concerns, albeit not directly addressed, were being heard. It also needs to be mentioned that the port authority, as stated before, did begin the construction of a new field that would do exactly what Armstrong's plan proposed without having the pilots stretch their machines through creative maneuvering by simply diverting the new field's location and direction. Unfortunately, the field was not yet finished by the time of the Elizabeth trilogy of disasters in the winter of 1951–52. Still, as the original airstrip did not yield any crashes prior to these events, we will never know if the new field would have simply supplemented the old one or if it would have replaced it, as it did after the crashes occurred. We also do not know if any inkling of the looming disasters would have sped up the already snail-paced construction of the new field.

When Governor Driscoll was asked in a resolution by the City of Newark to direct the Port Authority of New York to halt its already in-full-swing expansions in the summer of 1950, many, including Commissioner Ellenstein, were already pushing for a complete relocation of the airfield. Ellenstein's fight proved to be futile. The resolution rejected by the governor in favor of expanding the airstrips to accommodate jet airplanes did, however, bring to light some curious points about the airport and the original airfield still being used at the time of the tragedies. If nothing else, it at least uncovered the fact that the potential for such tragedies was openly discussed, even if ultimately ignored. The resolution pointed out that Newark Airport, when built twenty-three years prior, was designed for planes requiring eight-hundred-foot runways. The new runways being constructed and "extending into Elizabeth [were] 9,000 feet long."[53] Furthermore, the weight and horsepower of planes had increased 750 percent during the duration of the airport's existence. None of this was anticipated in the original plans. "It was beyond the realm of wildest imagination that aircraft of such greatly increased size and power would be utilized in the future," Ellenstein stated.[54] The commissioner was not the only one in this fight. When the city commission held a two-day hearing about the operation of Newark Airport by the Port Authority of New York, the testimonies lasted seven hours, with a barrage by thirty-two opposition speakers being given the floor during the duration of the opening session.[55] The opponents of the port authority's takeover and expansion of the airport hit mainly at the increased noise and diminishing quality of life caused by the expanded airport.

The resolution stressed the fact that the port authority had publicly spoken about trying to minimize the noise and low flying of the aircraft over heavily populated areas, but nothing had been done toward alleviating those problems. It called for the port authority and Newark Airport to once again be surveyed by the Civil Aeronautics Administration and a State of New Jersey–backed commission created for just such a purpose. The real intent came at the end of the document when it brought up the newly accepted modern planning of placing airports in areas remote from cities so that there would be no interference with large populations. Ellenstein even cited the example of Detroit relocating its municipal airport twenty-five miles from the city.[56] In retrospect, the idea of moving the airfields away from congested areas was, and still is, very difficult to put into action. As suburbs grew across the nation in the 1950s, it became nearly impossible to *find* remote areas near heavily congested city centers that were free from occupants. To the disappointment of Ellenstein and others fighting the airport, it seemed that the CAA already knew that.

The CAA continued to stress the safety of Newark Airport and pointed to the lack of incidents, which precluded it from changing its stance. After finishing its survey and study of the airport, as was requested by Governor Driscoll, the CAA steadfastly adhered to its initial opinions. All efforts to reduce plane noise and overhead flying had failed, and as numerous newspapers recounted, these "would not be stressed any longer, a Civil Aeronautics Administration official reported."[57] Ora W. Young, the regional administrator of the CAA, announced that the flight patterns adopted at the three fields in March 1949 were already designed to keep the noise of incoming and outgoing planes as far as possible from the residents and neighborhoods. He did admit that the airport would look into revisions—a story many Elizabeth and Newark folks had heard before.[58] As the final nail in the coffin, the CAA stated that the people's concerns of noise and low flights were the least of three basic considerations when it came to providing a seal of approval for airports. "The CAA," Young said, "has taken the stand that a traffic pattern, as is the case for all civil regulations, should be and will be enforced first, to achieve safety—safety in the air and on the ground; second, for most expeditious aircraft arrivals and departures, and third, noise abatement."[59] The CAA's answer to the concerned citizens and anti-airport politicians was summarized bluntly: "Until the quiet airplane becomes a

Gasoline loading and mechanics checking—routine parts of the service that made planes pass inspection for preflight. *Courtesy of Newark Public Library.*

reality our society must pay some price for the progress it has demanded and stimulated for high speed and comfortable aerial transportation."[60]

As for the calls of moving the airport farther away from the congested areas of Elizabeth and Newark altogether, the defense again pointed to the lack of fatal crashes or any safety issues—the latter not just with Newark Airport but also with other airports throughout the nation that were located near congested areas. The port authority taunted the opposition with claims of its airport being one of the most secure in the nation. In fact, the CAA maintained its stance on Newark Airport as one of the safest even *after* the first Elizabeth crash in December 1951—where it once again gave it a clean bill of health.[61] The CAA and the port authority, while highlighting the airfield's unsullied record, failed to stress the fatal accident that had occurred near the airport on September 13, 1932, when two people were killed in a moth-type plane that took off from its fields. The only other fatal accident connected to Newark Airport, twenty years prior to the Elizabeth tragedies, did not involve either of the Elizabeth or Newark neighborhoods. On that day in September, "baseball fans at the Newark Bears' Stadium saw a small plane abruptly nose down from an altitude of about 300 feet and drop like a rocket, plummeting into the soft muckland of the meadows."[62] As reported at the time by the *Herald News* of Passaic, New Jersey, the plane, carrying a pilot and student from the airport's flying school, "hit the soft ground with such an impact that it buried its nose, motor, and the two bodies more than six feet in the mud. When the first people arrived on the scene, only the shattered wings and the tail of the fuselage were visible."[63] In defense of the port authority and the CAA, this was indeed the only fatal accident in the airport's history. It was also not caused by the established flight patterns over the concerned neighborhoods but by student pilot error. Its exclusion from the CAA and port authority's reports, however, does raise some eyebrows when it comes to the otherwise spotless transparency record of the federal agency.

The official statements by the port authority defending the airport—even after the crash occurred—had also noted that sixty-two major airports in the United States had runways located closer to residential areas than Newark's. "The White House," the statement said, "is about the same distance from Washington National Airport as is the center of Elizabeth from Newark Airport."[64] Unbeknownst to the parties involved, and with the hindsight of additional seventy years of scientific study, the statements proclaiming the safety of living near airports were far from true—regardless of any crashes. The July 2015 study "Airports, Air Pollution, and Contemporaneous Health," by researchers out of Columbia University and supported by the Robert Wood Johnson Foundation, reported that "people who live within six miles [of an airport] have higher levels of asthma and heart problems caused by their higher exposure to carbon monoxide from planes."[65] Furthermore, the study points to a possible correlation between higher levels of anxiety and the proximity of living near airfields. Still, while providing a limitation to the airport's defense, the findings of a modern study cannot be used against the CAA mired by 1950s science and innovation. In fact, in the CAA's defense, and to establish its credibility at the time of the statements made against moving the airport, it does at least appear that it acted with pure intentions. Armed with the most up-to-date data analysis and knowledge, the agency's standards were not lax by any means. Thus, the approval by the Civil Aeronautics Administration was taken at face value. Even by the 1950s, before any plane could go into service, it had to be certified to ensure that there were no weaknesses in its structure or individual parts, no matter how minute they were. The physical inspection was followed by extensive testing by experts to uncover any indication of malfunction that could quickly be corrected to ensure safe operation. Even the crew was vetted by experts and certified to handle the type of aircraft flown. And if an accident did occur, a specified government agency moved in to discover the cause. New regulations were promptly instituted to prevent the same type of problem from repeating itself. Hence the thought of CAA's negligence being a cause of the Elizabeth tragedies would spur not only unwarranted conspiracy theories but also be unfair in light of all other evidence.

According to Knight, by 1958, there were more than 1,700 U.S. airliners of a dozen different types carrying passengers across the country and overseas under the strictest federal government observation. Equal supervision was also applied to the innumerable foreign carriers landing in the United States, as they also had to register for flyability. The two government agencies responsible for controlling the bursting air traffic were the Civil Aeronautics Administration and the Civil Aeronautics Board. While the former's responsibilities of enforcing flight safety and air traffic have already been covered, the latter began to play a larger role as the story of the three crashes evolved. The CAB, an independent agency that derived its power directly from Congress, acted with a quasi-judicial power when it came to initiating new legislative acts pertaining to air safety. It promulgated into law all U.S. civil air regulations under which all commercial aviation in the country operated. It also enforced all safety rules for all carriers of any sort and operated its own Bureau of Safety, which investigated and analyzed accidents.[66] It is the latter that we focus on when studying the events in New Jersey from the winter of 1951–52. One member of the CAB around the time of the accidents stated:

> *Our paramount objective is prevention. We try to learn not only from accidents but from minor troubles where there are no accidents. We don't want recurrences; we don't want the first one to happen. And the same goes for all segments of the industry (manufactures, fuel refineries, etc.). We get the fullest cooperation from all of them.*[67]

The organization prided itself, and rightfully so, on the results of its efforts to improve the safety of the public and aeronautical structure. When viewed in light of the tragedies, it becomes evident that both the CAA and the CAB followed all their established protocols and regulations that made them have the overall safety record that they had. It is this fact that makes the accidents in Elizabeth that much more difficult to comprehend.

The New Jersey trilogy of crashes occurred within a six-year period when the U.S. safety record was positively exemplary, especially when

Two workers unloading cargo from a car into an American Airlines plane at Newark Airport in preparation for flight. *Courtesy of Newark Public Library.*

considering the dangerous reality of flying. Between 1950 and 1956, there occurred fewer than one fatality per 100 million passenger miles flown, in contrast to about 2.5 per 100 million for private automobile travel; 0.21 per 100 million passenger miles in railroad transport; and about 0.40 per the same equation for buses.[68] Unfortunately, people do not focus on the countless safe flights as hundreds and thousands of airplanes fly unnoticed above them each day. Even for the people of Elizabeth and Newark, who would see, hear and feel each airplane that came near Newark Airport, they could not point to one other tragedy—apart from the already mentioned 1932 small plane incident. According to the director of flight safety research of the U.S. Air Force, speaking in 1956, the American military alone kept between 1,100 and 1,200 planes in the worldwide air twenty-four hours around the clock—all while sharing the airspace with an even greater number of commercial and private air carriers.[69] All of this before the safer jet airplanes came of age in the late 1950s and early 1960s. Both the CAA and the CAB agreed that air accidents involved both the occasional human error and the fallibility of working parts under extreme conditions—two things that would unfortunately forever be the weakness of advancing civilizations.[70]

The flying age was indeed an age of progress. Unfortunately, it was also the epitome of all the things that could go wrong. After all, it could easily have been human error, weather or structural failure that brought down the three planes on an already shaken and desperate population of Elizabeth, New Jersey. It could have even been all three—or none of them. There is still much to be debated, especially with many people still unable to fathom the circumstances of the three tragedies, even after official reports and explanations had been provided. After all, it was a tragedy that the government agencies tasked with solving it themselves would go on to call "unprecedented and strange." Unprecedented and strange indeed.

Chapter 3

WHEN PLANES STARTED FALLING

Sunday, December 16, 1951, was a cold day. People hurried their feet as they traversed the icy sidewalks, their heads down against the frigid wind. Nearby, children took advantage of the first real snow of the season as they pulled their sleighs behind them, laughing. Looking up into the windows, they could see families setting their tables for dinner. As if cutting through the serene winter afternoon, the loud noise of an aircraft labored through the skies—not an uncommon sound in the city of Elizabeth. Yet on that day, something seemed off. The noise was just that much louder than usual and the plane that much lower. Hundreds of feet below it, Bud Kessner, a World War II pilot, was following the plane as best as he could in his car. "I heard the pilot feather out," he later said, "I thought he'd be alright."[71] A few streets away, Abe Rosen, driving toward Newark Airport, noticed the plane. "It was really pulling hard and was just skimming above some trees. I turned to my wife, Miriam, and told her, 'that plane is in trouble. It's going to crash.'"[72] Bud, still following as best as he could, pressed on the brakes and pulled over to the side of the road: "[I]t burst into flames and the wing fell off, I knew then [the pilot] was a goner." Unfolding before them was the second-worst commercial plane disaster in U.S. history. Unbeknownst to the people of Elizabeth, they were about to be thrust into a surreal tragedy that would not let off for another fifty-eight days—still to be felt today, nearly seventy years later.

Fifteen-year-old Raymond J. Lamberti stepped off the bus just in time to look up at the disaster unfolding in front of him: "The motor blew. It toppled down, dropping very fast, and then the plane itself blew up as it hit the water."[73] Mrs. Maude Fellis, living one block away from the scene of the crash, watched hopelessly as the plane came directly at her home, just skimming above her roof. "I ran to the back window when I heard it," she said. "I think I went hysterical then." Speaking about it afterward, Maude recalled, "I thought there was only one boy in that plane, and I kind of think he hit the spot intentionally to save us."[74] Down below, children screamed in panic as they abandoned their sleighs and ran for home—a flaming monster looming above them. "I screamed and screamed," said an eight-year-old girl who lived just one block away from the crash. "I was scared."[75] Ms. Laura Angen, another eyewitness to the tragedy, later recalled, "I was about to say to my baby 'Look at the plane' when I saw smoke coming from its rear end. As it made a full turn toward Newark airport, it was blazing on the side. It was very low. I could see it was trying to land," she added.[76] Joseph Dwyer and his brother, Roy, at the time thirteen and twelve, respectively, spoke of seeing the stricken plane coming right toward their father's chicken farm in nearby Union City, New Jersey. "Flames were coming around the body when it came down low. When it went [past us], it just cleared the woods."[77] Then came the big *thud*.

This photo of the first crash was snapped by a Union, New Jersey resident from the front window of his house. *From the* Herald News *(Passaic), December 17, 1951.*

"I ran down Westfield Avenue, and I saw wide sheets of flames enveloping the Elizabethtown Water Co. warehouse," recounted Lou Mogelever, a *Newark Star Ledger* reporter who had just settled down to have a cigar with his friends when he heard the crash. "The plane was a jumbled mass of metal and was burning fiercely. It landed on top of a large rubbish pile." As more and more people arrived at the scene, the reporter recalled an eerie "silence…a cold silence everywhere."[78] A scene of dichotomy ensued as the silence of the shocked citizens was broken by faint noises coming from the wreckage. "I heard cries from inside the plane," said Bill Kapio of Union City, "but I didn't know what to do."[79] The would-be rescuers, held back by the intense heat coming off the wreckage, could not believe the striking contrast of what was unfolding before them as they battled with their firehoses and water freezing in the subzero weather. "The first thing they carried out was a little bit of a baby, real small, wrapped in a blanket. I saw pieces of clothing and part of a person's body lying over on one side and part of a body lying close to the tail of the plane," recalled the teenage Lamberti to a local reporter.[80] The child's remains were followed by what seemed like countless bodies being inched up the icy ravine next to the wreckage. At the top, they were set in a row, a grisly line of blackened, torn bodies.[81] The mayor and the city councilmen hurried to the snowy ravine, where they were seen lifting the bodies out of the wreckage and hauling them up to the top. It seemed like the whole town turned out to help. Ambulances and an old bus were tasked with moving the bodies to the funeral home, which also served as the Elizabeth morgue. The fifty-six bodies had to be laid out in the garage behind the mortuary, as there simply was not enough room for them in the main building. There was a total of forty-eight adult passengers on the plane, two children, two infants, the pilot, two copilots and a stewardess. Many were leaving for their winter vacations, planning to spend their Christmas holidays in Florida on the Miami-bound flight.[82] The death toll of fifty-six people in the Elizabeth plane crash was topped by only one other commercial disaster in the nation's history, a New York–Minneapolis airliner that plunged into Lake Michigan on June 24, 1930, with a loss of fifty-eight lives. Being the scene of the second-worst plane crash in the nation was not a distinction the people of Elizabeth, New Jersey, wanted to be known for.

Robert Collins—who put his mother, his sister and two infant nephews on the doomed plane for a holiday vacation in Tampa—described the plane's troubled takeoff at Newark Airport. Speaking through sobs and tears, Collins recalled, "Every seat was taken. We had been at the airport since early morning for the scheduled takeoff. But there was a delay, and an airline official said the heaters were not working. Finally, about three o'clock, the plane took off."[83] Robert kissed his mother and stepped off the plane—the last person to do so. Minutes later, his family, to whom he just said goodbye, were all dead. As the CAA and the CAB descended on the scene and local newspapers attempted to re-create the events of December 16, one sentiment was universal. The pilot had died fighting the controls of the crippled plane, trying to avoid hitting numerous homes, concurrently saving as many lives as possible. In the end, his plane clipped only one unoccupied house before smashing into an unused water pumping station

One of the first pictures to be published of the aftermath of the first crash from December 1951. *Courtesy of Newark Public Library.*

on the banks of the Elizabeth River. Captain Albert C. Lyons of Miami was lauded for avoiding an even bigger catastrophe. State Senator Kenneth C. Hand said on the scene, "It was only a miracle that hundreds of people weren't killed….The plane missed apartment houses by a small fraction."[84] J.P. Ward, an owner of a parking lot directly next to the crash site, perhaps summarized what everyone in Elizabeth was thinking: "The pilot ought to have a place in heaven for trying to save [us]."[85] Another resident added, "I kind of think he hit the spot intentionally to save us."[86] A man who was mere feet away from the crash and miraculously survived later said, "My wife said that pilot is a hero. I believe her. This is a very crowded section, and he crashed the plane into the only place in this area where there were no houses packed together."[87]

For those aboard the two-engine C-46 passenger plane, Florida would have been a good escape from the frigid temperatures of New Jersey that December. Operated by a non-scheduled company, the Miami Airlines plane came into Newark Airport from Fort Smith, Arkansas, at about midnight on December 16, 1951. As was the case with all incoming flights, it then went through routine maintenance and was deemed safe and ready for its next flight to Miami at 10:00 a.m. the same day. An examination

December 17, 1951 crash. Firemen are seen bringing bodies out of the icy Elizabeth River Ravine. *From the* Courier News, *December 17, 1951.*

Newspapers in New Jersey were very similar on December 17, 1951. Here is the front page of the *Bergen Evening Record*, December 17, 1951.

The scene of the first crash, showing the debris along the industrial stretch of the Elizabeth River. The icy ravine up which the bodies were dragged up can be seen on the right. *Courtesy of Newark Public Library.*

of the manifest later showed that the craft's weight had exceeded by 117 pounds the maximum load allowance decreed by CAB regulations—though not enough to prevent the flight from proceeding as scheduled.[88] The non-scheduled flight cost $39.74, a little more than half the price of a seat aboard a regularly scheduled airline. The aircraft, originally scheduled to take off in the morning, was delayed five hours while repairs were made to its heating system. As reported by newspapers at the time, Captain R.W. Duff, the president of the line, said that the plane was purchased as surplus from the air force after World War II, having logged four thousand hours since then.[89] On that fateful day, the old plane was in trouble from the very start, before it even cleared the runway.

An eyewitness said that a cloud of black smoke fanned out from behind one of its engines as the plane began racing down the runway. "The right engine on the plane was smoking very badly on the takeoff and it took the whole length of the field before it rose about 50 feet," said another.[90] As the smoking plane raced down the runway, airport officials sprang into action.

Reports came in of one emergency truck smashing through a gate at the end of the field in its attempt to follow the falling plane. Everything was happening at lightning speed. Sensing his trouble, the pilot radioed back to the airport that he was returning. He promptly swung his craft around to try and make it back. Down below, instructions to crash landing crews from the control tower had already sent them into action. "Get out on the field. Stay off the runway," the orders said. "Craft taking off to the west with a smoking right engine. He's coming in on six. He is on fire."[91] In nearby Elizabeth, Tom Mulligan watched the plane from his front yard as it went into its final death plunge. "I saw the motor burning and heard an explosion which ripped the plane's right wing off and sent it boomeranging toward the left and crashing at a terrific speed."[92] Forty-nine-year-old Walter Bruns, a commercial telegrapher, was wheeling wood to his home on the river slope when the plane crashed one hundred feet away from him. "It was the worst thing I've ever seen," he said. "I looked up and saw this huge flaming mass coming down on me. I dropped the wood and ran across the street towards some kids who were sledding [yelling at them to get down].…When it hit the brick waterworks, a terrific roar came out. The kids were screaming, but I couldn't hear them."[93]

WITH REPORTERS AND PHOTOGRAPHERS kept out by Elizabeth Police, the first long-faced relatives of the crash victims began reporting to the morgue. It was December 17, 1951, one day after the crash. The bitter cold did not let off. Those present did not mind. Their scarfs, hats and coats pulled up high on their faces shielded their grief. The local chapter of the Red Cross was tasked with helping the identification of the "mangled bodies laid out like so much blackened cord wood."[94] Some that arrived were directed to the main building, others to the garage behind it and some even to a neighbor's garage pressed into the grim service since there simply was not enough room in the morgue to handle all of the bodies. James Stefanelli of Newark arrived to identify his brother.[95] With grief painted on his face, the young man came out of the morgue looking sick. He paced up and down the sidewalk, fighting away tears. He went in again only to come right out, unable to contain his sobs. It is not known if he found his brother that day. As reported by the authorities, many of the bodies were so badly mutilated that it would be impossible to identify them except by jewelry, personal effects, dental work and fingertips.[96] In the next few days, local dentists would be called to the scene to help with the identification process.

Rescue workers search for bodies in the overturned wreckage of the giant Florida-bound airplane. *From the Central New Jersey Home News (New Brunswick), December 17, 1951.*

Back at the ruined pump house into which the plane had crashed, a couple of local police officers stood nearby. They were not part of the cleanup crew or the investigation. They were there to guard the pitiful remains of the passengers' personal effects, which were collected and laid out inside the building. Past the door they were guarding was a cold room with concrete walls and a concrete floor. The sparingly placed naked lightbulbs hanging from old wooden beams illuminated the items covering every inch of the ground. There was a package with "handle with care" scribbled on it; a pair of binoculars, never to be used again to spot a winning horse at a Florida racetrack; and a box of heat-tarnished cufflinks nobody would get a chance to wear to Christmas dinner.[97] Shoes spilled out of broken luggage spread out throughout the room. Christmas gifts of lingerie were wrapped in cheerful paper. These and more would soon take on a bigger meaning, as they would play an important role in identifying some of the victims. Outside, the two police officers stood motionless and silent. They understood the significance of their assignment.

The fight against Newark Airport and the Port Authority of New York resumed with fervor almost instantly. State Senator Kenneth C. Hand was quoted in a newspaper the day after the accident: "Maybe this will make the Civil Aeronautics Authority realize that you can't have airports so close to heavily congested cities."[98] The same article pointed out the threat made by many of Elizabeth's residents when they spoke of forming a human barrier with their bodies to block the airport runway unless something was done. Stephen Moran, the city commissioner of Newark, ordered a survey to determine whether operations at Newark Airport were a "health menace" to local residents.[99] If the survey results came back in the affirmative, he promised that he would ask the city commission to start legal proceedings to shut down the airport. The survey—like the prior complaints about the airport being too close to the cities of Elizabeth and Newark—did not yield any support from the CAA. Within days after the tragedy, officials of seven municipalities were demanding a no-punches-pulled Congressional investigation of Newark Airport aimed at forcing its transfer to a less populous area. A subcommittee designated and bound for Washington, D.C., was formed and tasked with pressing the city's demands at the capital. It was a unified front, one called on by the mayors and civic leaders of the municipalities of Newark, Elizabeth, Hillside, Linden, Cranford, Roselle Park and Union. "We don't want our people living under an umbrella of constant fear," said Elizabeth's mayor, James T. Kirk.[100]

The group, calling themselves the "Mayor's Committee," initially asked for a probe of what they described as "health hazards caused by the around the clock drone of planes landing and taking off at Newark Airport."[101] The request was changed to a full-scale inquiry into the operations at the big airport and all aspects of the Port Authority of New York, its controlling body. Furthermore, an official letter was sent to Governor Driscoll to veto all attempts by the port authority to expand any airport facilities. Concurrent with the action of the newly created board was the start of the official probe into the nature and cause of the crash by six different agencies. It was on the findings of these twenty-three officials—working for/with the agencies on the federal, state and local level—that the fate of the airfield hung. At least, that was what the Mayor's Committee hoped. The investigators represented Elizabeth police, Union County, the New Jersey Bureau of Aeronautics, Essex County (where Newark Airport was located), the Civil Aeronautics Board and the Civil Aeronautics Administration.[102]

The investigation, which took a few weeks and culminated with more than sixty people being questioned, led to some conclusive (and yet also inconclusive) revelations. While many people saw the plane's engine on fire on takeoff, the investigation sided with the control tower operators' testimony that the plane's right engine was out of their line of vision prior to liftoff.[103] William J. Barner, a baggage man at Newark Airport, testified at the Civil Aeronautics Board hearing that he noticed oil leaking from the right engine of the doomed plane. The man sat with his head looking at the ground when asked why he had not reported the leak. "Because it happens so often," he replied in what amounted to a whisper.[104] A pilot and copilot who were passengers on the plane the day before the disaster both testified that they

The front page of the December 17, 1951 *New York Daily News* put it bluntly.

noticed no disorder with the plane during their trip, except that there was little heat in the cabin.[105] There were some other notable findings from the testimonies that, although standing out in the report, did not necessarily add to solving the cause of the crash. It was reported that the pilot of the doomed plane had previously been served with a complaint by the CAA that could have resulted in the revocation or suspension of his license. Furthermore, it was revealed that between February 1947 and September 1950, Miami Airline Inc., the operator of the two-engine C-46 airliner, paid a total of $1,800 in fines to the CAA on sixteen charges of rule violations, consisting mostly of overloading its planes to Puerto Rico and Florida.[106] Still, both charges were discarded as the cause of the crashed plane. The manifest showed the plane just slightly overweight, and the pilot's actions on that day were uniformly praised by all.

The final classification of the crash was deemed as "Loss of Control." As for the probable cause, the CAB determined that it was an unavoidable mechanical malfunction. "A stall with the landing gear extended following a serious loss of power from the right engine. This loss of power was caused by the failure of the hold-down studs of the no. 10 cylinder, precipitating a fire in flight which became uncontrollable."[107] Case closed.

As the indignation on the ground continued, so did the work on the new runway at Newark Airport. Numerous assurances graced the pages of the local papers that the new construction would lead to less noise and a lessened chance of future accidents. The proponents of closing and/or moving the airport had once again been rebuffed by the CAA and the CAB, both of which found no fault on the part of the Port Authority of New York and that of its giant airport in having any part in the crash. Ironically, the investigators sought to soothe airport foes by declaring that this was a "once in a lifetime" tragedy and that it "could never happen again."[108] Like the inevitable cold of the winter of 1951–52, the airport and low flyovers were there to stay. As weeks went by and 1951 turned into 1952, many people would never forget the events of that fateful day: the screaming children running for cover, charred bodies of babies being taken out of the plane's wreckage and local priests administering last rites in ice-cold waters on the banks of the Elizabeth River with nothing but floodlights guiding their way. Little did they know that they had lived through just the first chapter of a three-scene tragedy.

Chapter 4

THE TWENTIETH PLANE IN TWO HOURS

It was January 23, 1952, a little over a month since the last crash. Planes continued to fly above the heads of weary Elizabeth and Newark citizens. It was a Tuesday, midafternoon. A vacant lot sat at the corner of South Street and Williamson Street. There were two wooden apartment houses bordering the lot on each side—one on each street. In the house on South Street, a Greek Orthodox priest, making his traditional post-Christmas calls, had come to bless the house.[109] The holy man raised his right hand and began to speak. At that moment, a plane hit the other house, less than one hundred feet away on Williamson Street. *The Record* interviewed many witnesses just hours after the holocaust. A towheaded five-year-old who lived next to the brick apartment house shuttered by the crash, looking up at the reporter with eyes wide open, proclaimed in his little voice, "My name is James Gregory Kasper, and [I think] the airplane had two guns."[110] A tired old man looked up from under the rain-soaked brim of his hat to listen to someone read off the name of the pilot. "That's him. That's my son-in-law."[111] In the same building that little Mr. Kasper lived in, gasoline flames continued to devour the structure. In the kitchen, in the rear of the second floor, stood a little girl no older than seven. She stood as if frozen in time. She listened to the growing sounds of three men dashing up the stairs to help her mother, her grandmother and her baby sister down to safety.[112] From the comfort of the man's arms carrying her out of the building, she quietly glanced at the bubbling, smoking ruins around her. Pieces of furniture, photographs in frames lay unnaturally twisted by the heat, and then an alien object in her house: a piece of a propeller covered in mud from the dirt and firemen's hoses.[113]

American Airlines Convair flight no. 6780, on a scheduled run to Newark Airport, was coming in from its last stop in Syracuse with a crew of three and twenty passengers. Among them that afternoon was a former secretary of war Robert P. Patterson, a driving force behind pioneering early flight and today best remembered as the man instrumental in creating the famous African American fighter group known as the Tuskegee Airmen. Captain Thomas J. Reid, a World War II flight veteran, radioed Newark tower when he was coming over neighboring Linden and asked for guidance from the ground. The fog and rain that day had limited Reid's visibility to less than three-fourths of a mile.[114] Even with the near-freezing temperatures, the exchange of information between the pilot and the flight control operators on the ground, guiding the craft into position for a routine ILS (instrument landing system) landing, made it all seemed routine enough. In the two hours immediately preceding the Convair's approach, nineteen other planes landed or took off safely on the assigned Newark runway for which Reid was headed.[115] Flight 6780 would not be the twentieth.

When still five and a half miles out, Reid was told that his position was about nine hundred feet to the left off course. Later, he was again warned he was "a trifle off course and high," and while he was over Elizabeth and three and a half miles away from the runway, he was now "drifting to the right and 900 feet beyond the glide-path"—an easily corrected error where an aircraft is still about one thousand feet high.[116] None of this caused any concern or alarm. In fact, the drifting of an airplane to correct the guide pattern was pretty standard. The plane's ceiling was down to four hundred feet, and visibility still cut to nearly half of a mile as the plane headed for the airport's Runway 6. The radar controller at the Newark Airport tower continued monitoring the incoming craft until it was roughly half a mile south of the Union County Courthouse in Elizabeth.[117] The ILS system guiding the plane down was a recent invention developed by the Civil Aeronautics Administration and was designed to permit a pilot to see whether he was on the proper approach path to an airport by watching two

Captain Thomas Reid, the pilot of the American Airlines Convair of the January 22, 1952 crash. *From the* New York Daily News, *January 23, 1952.*

needles on an indicator. The *Herald News* of Passaic, New Jersey, days after the accident, brought up the point that the system was not designed to bring a plane down to airport runways at the time of its invention. Its main job was to enable the pilot to break through overcast skies to a position where he could see well enough to make a visual landing. That same article also noted that there had been "documented cases of airport radar sets blanking out because of heavy rain."[118]

As the young man in the control tower took his eyes off the blinking screen for one second, by the time he looked back as if through magic, the plane had disappeared from his radar. It was 3:45 p.m. All calls sent out to the aircraft came back unanswered. The thoughts of the man sitting at the desk began racing back to just eight days prior, when a Northeastern Airliner, also a two-engine Convair like the one that just disappeared from his radar screen, undershot the neighboring LaGuardia Field and crashed into the East River in New York City. And even though all thirty-five people aboard that plane were rescued, it did not deter him from fearing for the worse.[119] He quickly dismissed his concerns. After all, it would be impossible for another plane to crash in Elizabeth within a single month.

The plane came out of the clouds, hedgehopping over Elizabeth's homes. It was losing ground and heading directly toward Battin High School. Going over another school and a hospital on its troubled approach, the aircraft sheared off the roof and the upper structure of a brick building, demolished a two-story garage that had been converted into a home and slammed into a house near the high school.[120] The final resting place was roughly two hundred yards away from the school, where one thousand girls had been released from classes a short forty-five minutes earlier and where many teachers remained preparing for the next day.[121] "We looked out a window and saw buildings burst into flames," said a faculty member of Battin High School. "People came running out into the street. One woman was screaming, 'My baby is in there!'"[122] As flames engulfed the apartment home and the nearby three-story brick building, the would-be rescue workers stood anxiously after being halted in place by the intense heat. As reported later, it was a full ninety minutes before the raging, gasoline-fed flames allowed anyone near the buildings. Screaming residents ran for safety. During that time, firemen and police watched in disbelief and hoped that the flames would not make true their threat to spread to the entire block. Just across Williamson Street was the nearby missed school. Across the playground was St. Mary's High School, and less than a block away was St. Elizabeth Hospital. "As the plane hit one building, it immediately disintegrated into a mass of bricks and fire. Seconds later, the house next door was all in flames," said twenty-nine-year-old high school art teacher Michael Truss, who witnessed the plane hit.[123]

"There was a terrific explosion," said Mrs. Ann Wurth, a nearby resident. "I picked up my boy and ran as far away as I could go."[124] As the rain pelted down the flames, one could not escape the smell of smoke and burning rubber and the steam that seemed to fill the air. "I'll never forget the screams of the dying. I was there in a minute, but I couldn't do anything. The flames…." Peter Lesniak, a foundry worker, wrung his hands and wiped the rain from his face as he tried to talk to the reporters. With a frenzy of police, firemen and news media swarming around the still-hot debris right behind him, he added, "It [is] a miracle any of the people got out of those houses. I know many of them, and I couldn't help them."[125] Ironically, low-flying planes continued to roar down over the scene of the tragedy, often drowning out the statements that local reporters tried to take from witnesses. The commotion was intense. Later recollections pointed to the red lights blinking on fire trucks and ambulances, water shooting from fire hoses mixing with the heavy rain, and endless screams. The first litter bearers began to bring out the bodies, asking the onlookers and reporters to let them pass as they made their way through the mud-soaked ground and debris. "Wet blankets covered the bodies. The forms of legs, heads, and torsos could be made out. One was of a very pot-bellied man…over in another spot, four men were picking up pieces of a body and putting them on a rubber-sheeted stretcher."[126]

The plane crashed next to somebody's corner lot garden. The entire property was ground into a swamp of slimy, soft mud by the hundreds of feet and car tires. It took boards and such to create a walkable path. Rod Odell, a *Herald News* staff writer, recalled the next day, "There was a clutter of blanket-covered forms lying behind a house. They were in thick mud. I counted a dozen. I turned away. When I looked back, there were 13… unlucky number. The rain pelted the blankets and they got wet and seemed almost to cling to the forms underneath."[127] The disaster units that answered the emergency call included the same crews that worked on the last Elizabeth crash, one month and one mile away from their current task. One of the many volunteers who helped at the scene that day was Don Newcombe, star hurler for the Brooklyn Dodgers, who also happened to be a member of the nearby Colonia Volunteer Fire Department.[128] A policeman recalled twenty-one-year-old Carmen Venezia dashing into one of the buildings and coming out with a woman as well as that woman's daughter and grandchild.[129] The

The aftermath of the second crash, on January 23, 1952. The plane hit a home on Williamston Street, killing four people inside it. *Courtesy of Newark Public Library.*

same newspaper article spoke of two unidentified patrolmen rescuing Mrs. Rose Caruso from her flame- and smoke-filled kitchen by crawling through a mass of wreckage to reach her. As the recovered bodies were placed on wooden planks hastily set down on a sea of red mud, Reverend John Meyer of St. Mary's Church intoned the last rites of his church.[130]

Initially, the crowds were not large, and newspapers reported a few hundred standing about, outside of the fire line ropes. But after the supper hour, the crowds picked up "to perhaps a thousand or two."[131] There was an eerie glare of the many lights brought to illuminate the rescuers' efforts. One large fragment of the airplane wing, sheared off and discarded by the impact, rested on the ground near the commotion. It seemed like that was all that was left from the airplane, with the rest transforming and disappearing into the jumbled wreckage of what was once a home. Among the shattered bits of furniture, a washing machine, a TV set and children's toys, a dazed Albert Ragone, thirty-four, could be seen wandering about. He came home from work to find his home in ruins and his wife and two young sons missing.[132]

American Airlines Convair CV-240 crashes into a home on January 22, 1952. The pilot claimed visibility issues shortly before disappearing from radar screens. *Courtesy of Newark Public Library.*

"I cannot find them," he kept repeating. Within hours of the airplane crash, the rescue workers, with their heads down to shield them from the shelling and relentless rain, had recovered most of the bodies. As brave as they all were, none had the strength left in them to inform Albert that his wife and two sons, three years and fourteen months, had been found. The young wife and her two children would never again meet Al at the dinner table when he came home. More than one hundred miles away in Darby, Pennsylvania, Mrs. Ann Siegle rushed her older daughter to the Pennsylvania Hospital for a major surgical operation. As she prayed for her daughter's life in the waiting room, a police officer in Elizabeth had just placed the mangled body of her younger daughter on the wet, mud-stained planks in the empty lot between the destroyed buildings.[133] Marilyn Ruth Siegel, voted the prettiest girl in her class at Springfield High School in Philadelphia, loved the sense of adventure her new job as an American Airlines stewardess awarded her.[134] She was twenty-one.

Carol Golison, a nineteen-year-old Syracuse University student from Somerville, New Jersey, sat motionless as the call of the disaster came through. She missed the plane home while finishing a mid-year exam.[135] Her four friends made the flight and became four casualties of the twenty-eight dead—twenty-one of whom were passengers of the American Airlines plane. Reportedly, the eighteen passengers, three crew members and two company personnel aboard the plane were burned beyond recognition. Seven bodies were brought out from the houses impacted by the crash, and at least eleven other people were injured, nine of them in their homes. On that fateful Tuesday, Sheila Earlman, eight, and Donna Mandel, seven, went to Donna's house after school to play with their dolls. The following day, one lay dead and the other badly burned—victims of the airplane that exploded into the house.[136] Long after Sheila was taken to the hospital with her mother and little sister, her best friend, Donna, was still missing. Even after rescuers located her little body in the rubble of what was once her home, it took days before anyone had the heart to tell Sheila.

The Associated Press reported that the flood of telephone calls in the wake of the plane crash forced the New Jersey Bell Telephone Company to install manual service at Elizabeth Police Station, firehouse and hospitals, enabling them to select incoming calls and to make outside calls with a minimum delay.[137] With the sun coming up on another cold January morning, the lives of many families would never return to normal. Apart from the macabre "coincidence" of a plane crashing in a near exact spot within the same month, the incident received unprecedented news coverage due to the select few passengers that had been on board. Among the eighteen passenger victims was John F. Chester, forty-five, former general business editor for the Associated Press and a World War II war correspondent. There were also two CAA officials on the plane: George T. Williams, chief of the CAA's navigational aids section, and John D. Rice, acting chief of the radar group.[138] Yet by far the most recognized name from the casualties was former secretary of war Robert P. Patterson, who perhaps prophetically remarked only a month prior to a room full of patrons at a dinner event that his death might come unexpectedly.[139] Patterson, who was in Buffalo, New York, for a court case, had not planned to leave until nighttime and had already secured a train ticket. However, when his case finished earlier, he canceled his train ticket and instead asked his associate to secure a plane reservation instead. "My personal loss is tremendous," proclaimed President Truman. "Our country has lost a man who understood with all his mind and heart the true meaning of our form of government and our way of

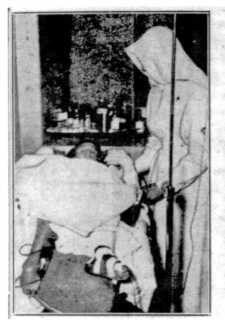

Above: An injured Sheila Earlman, eight, is treated at St. Elizabeth's Hospital while her mother is comforted in the waiting room after the second crash. *From the* New York Daily News, *January 23, 1952.*

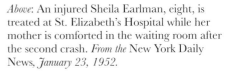

Left: Newspaper insert following the second crash as it appeared in Hackensack's *The Record*—former secretary of war Robert P. Patterson (*top left*); John Chester (*top right*), former editor of the Associated Press; Captain Thomas J. Reid (*bottom left*); and stewardess Marilyn Ruth Siegel (*bottom right*). *From* The Record, *January 23, 1952.*

life and who was willing to fight for them with all the great gifts God gave him."[140] For the first time, the proponents of a fight against Newark Airport and the Port Authority of New York had the national attention they needed. The fight, which was already in full swing after the last airplane crash from the month prior, was given an extra boost, albeit at the cost of yet another tragedy. Yet, as before, the anti–Newark Airport movement would taste the bitterness of bureaucracy.

An immediate investigation was launched into the cause of the crash by Joseph O. Fluet, regional director of the Civil Aeronautics Board, the same man who had just days prior completed a probe of the Miami-bound C-46 that crashed in Elizabeth one month earlier. By 10:00 a.m., the morning after the crash, Fluet was joined by Elizabeth Police, the New Jersey Aeronautics Board and the CAA. This was becoming too much of a routine for many of those present—more than it should ever have been. Meanwhile, before the investigation ever really got underway, American Airlines had already flooded the local papers with defensive statements that its planes had flown 4,619,000,000 passenger miles without a fatality since its last fatal accident at Dallas, Texas, three years before, where twenty-eight people were killed.[141] Also from Washington came a report that the crash of the day before was the first fatal accident a Convair airplane had since that model was put into service almost four years earlier.[142] None of this was of any consolation to the family members who lined up at the same Elizabeth morgue that barely handled the last tragedy. They were there once again to try to identify the twenty-eight unfortunate victims of this new catastrophe. Like the fifty-six victims of the month prior, the mutilated bodies were laid out in the two-car garage of the Haines Funeral Home. Dr. George W. Horre, the county physician, said that ten of the victims were identified exclusively through dental records up to that point. Other personal effects were still waiting to be found and brought into the funeral place. This was because the digging in the house and plane wreckage was temporarily halted to permit CAB investigators' preliminary examinations.[143]

Angry shouts characterized the "indignation meeting" in the city council chamber of Elizabeth two days after the second accident in thirty-seven days rocked one of the state's largest cities.[144] A resolution was adopted calling for a full-scale investigation of the airport's plans and operations. The demands for either the immediate closing of the airfield or a ban on flights over the city could not be ignored. More than five hundred people overcrowded the room, packing aisles and the corridor of a chamber that only held three hundred seats. Many of those present said they did not want Elizabeth to become known as "the world's number one disaster city."[145] The meeting began with a minute of silence in memory of the twenty-eight victims of the January 22 crash. Deputy Attorney General Nelson F. Stamler opened the meeting with the following words:

I come here as a citizen of the community—not as an official of the state. I too, and my family, have been plagued by the planes. I've been sickened by the recent crashes. I think it is wonderful for the city council of Elizabeth to make the first solid step toward some cure of what I deem to be pure criminal negligence. I don't think the deaths the other night were anything but sheer murder.[146]

Council President John C. Boyle followed, telling the crowd that he was "heartsick and trembling with fear that it could have happened to me and my family."[147]

Newark's mayor, Ralph A. Villani, leveled his own blast against the airport. "I think we've had enough," he said. "The airport must go. It is too close to a large population for anyone's safety." He then added that he had instructed the Corporation Counsel to find any legal means to get rid of it—even "to searching for technical flaws in Newark's lease with the New York Port Authority for the field."[148] In anticipation of the fight before them and before the meeting even took place, the port authority had announced some temporary fixes as it worked on a more permanent solution. The people at the meeting balked at the new taxiway to be opened in the following weeks to help divert about 35 to 40 percent of all flight operations over barren marshland or surrounding water areas.[149] This measure was on top of a newly proposed instrument runway that would fix the problem once and for all by diverting all incoming planes in bad weather from the instrument flight path (which they were then taking over Elizabeth). Still, there were no words spoken about completely abandoning the current instrument runway, only about supplementing it. Perhaps more importantly, there was no talk about moving the airport altogether. As if speaking of a premonition, Councilman Thomas Dunn ended the meeting with, "The first tragedy—they looked for excuses. The second—they will try to explain. But a third would be murder."[150] Unnervingly poignant words, considering most of those present would be in the very same room, discussing the very same topic just a few weeks later after a third plane fell on Elizabeth.

As Senate investigators arrived in Newark on January 25, 1952, to study the airport's operations in connection with the two Elizabeth crashes, they were met with a flurry of FBI agents and Newark police personnel. They were there to search the airport and the administration buildings for a potential bomb. Earlier that day, a tip was called into the Elizabeth Police Station, claiming that the buildings and all the people in charge of the airport would be blown up. With guards set up around the buildings and no explosives found, the Senate investigators conferred with other Federal and Union County authorities already probing the disasters. The goal was to bring back as much information to Washington as they could. Following the airport inspection, the Senate investigators and a five-man House subcommittee that joined them visited the scene of the recent tragedies. While touring the crash sites, the men spoke candidly to reporters about ordering a thorough inspection of Newark Airport at the hands of the House Interstate Commerce Committee. They promised that all phases of its traffic would be studied before the final report would make its way back to the Capitol. Knowing what was heading his way in Washington, Charles F. Horne, Civil Aeronautics administrator, said that the airport's landing aid and procedures "fully met" CAA regulations and safety standards.[151] This was not going to be an easy fight. It was now up to the probes, spearheaded by the CAB, to determine the airport's fault, which could finally provide a victory for the anti-airport supporters. The federal government, which had complete control over interstate aviation, would rely on its agencies' thorough investigation to make the ultimate call to order any changes to Newark's airport.

By the time the final verdict in the second crash in Elizabeth was finally published, the third crash had already occurred. And although Newark Airport was by then temporarily shut down as a result of the final catastrophe, the CAB findings on the second crash did not provide the final nail in the coffin that the anti-airport proponents needed in order to keep the airport's planes grounded forever. In fact, it could be said that the report, which freed the airport and the Port Authority of New York from any wrongdoing in the second crash, just as it had in the first, helped with its eventual reopening to air traffic. According to CAB File No. 1-0016, "The Board determines that there is insufficient evidence at this time upon which to predicate a probable cause."[152] The report stated that when the plane left Buffalo, New York, it was carrying less than the allowable gross weight, as per CAA regulations; it also noted that evidence disclosed that all radio contacts with the flight of the airliner were normal before the crash and that "all compulsory position reports were made."[153] The aircraft's fuel supply was clean of any water particles, with no indication of the plane's engines having any malfunction or failure. Perhaps most importantly for those having to live with planes flying over their heads near Newark Airport, the board also said that the crash should not be attributed to improper functioning of the airport's landing guiding systems "because [they] functioned properly before and after the accident as well as during the subsequent exhaustive tests."[154] Last but not least, the report also eliminated weather as a contributing factor.

In all but direct wording, the accident was deemed a fluke. As for the fact that a plane had once again crashed into the city of Elizabeth, out of all places, it was explained simply as a weird coincidence. Both assertions were nowhere near good enough for the families of the countless lives lost and those who did not yet know they were living out their last days, as airplanes were not yet done falling on Elizabeth.

Chapter 5

"CAN'T MAKE IT BACK"

T he picture shows an elderly gentleman bending down over what appears to be a person. Standing above him are a police officer, a firefighter and a medic. Fifteen minutes earlier, with household belongings scattered in all directions around him, the man, with a heavy coat buttoned right up to his chin, held his hand on his mouth as he walked. Perhaps it was because of the cold, the fog, the sleet or the rain. Or perhaps it was the scene around him that made him continuously hold his breath. As he approached the officer, the sober-faced veteran pointed to the ground. The priest unbuttoned his coat. His hands were searching; they finally found what they were looking for. With the Bible and Rosary secure in his left hand, the elderly gentleman bent down to administer the last rites. He raised his right hand in the sign of the cross, not noticing the young man fidgeting with his camera just a few feet away.

The young reporter looked on silently, peering into the men's faces—those who leaned over the charred bodies of the victims of a second airplane crash in mere weeks. He felt that he saw past their despair, their anguish and their disbelief. More so than their silence, their actions spoke to him in volumes of the human impulse of empathy, kindness, caring and courage. Unspeakable tragedies such as those witnessed in Elizabeth in the previous weeks tended to be mourned and remembered for the pain and suffering of those involved. The young man knew the significance of his job as a photojournalist. He knew that memorializing the two tragedies would become a respectful way to honor those who had lost their lives. Yet, he also knew that his work could do something more. It could remind those left behind of something often

The only surviving photo of a priest bending over the bodies from the second crash to administer last rites as police and firemen stand in disbelief. *From the* Courier News *(Bridgewater, NJ), January 23, 1952.*

forgotten: that one can always find the light of human compassion even in the darkest of times. The priest was finishing his prayer—firemen, police officers and medics hovered behind him.

Rushing to capture the moment, the young man forgot to prime the bulb on his camera. Yet tonight, he did not really need to. There was plenty of light between the fire, the flashlights and the spotlights. He pressed the shutter button. *Click*. He did not know if the picture had come out. Ironically, he would not yet know that even if it had not, he would be given another chance at getting his shot just a short number of days later.

THREE WEEKS LATER...

Nancy Taylor opened her eyes. The world was upside down. No, she was upside down—held in place by her seatbelt. She later recalled sitting in the stewardess jump seat. "I couldn't see the passengers at all in the forward compartment. Before I knew it, everything was black...everything was crumbling."[155] It was dark in the cabin, almost pitch black. There were "moans, groans and crying" coming from behind her. Someone rushed in and tried talking to her, asking if she was all right. She could not decipher his words. As she struggled uncontrollably with her seatbelt, the man helped her unfasten it and led her down. The man moved ahead to assist others with the same endeavor. Nancy, still disoriented, crawled out of a hole where the front portion of the plane would have been. She fell, not remembering how many feet. Someone helped her up. As she looked back, she could see a great cloud of smoke and houses on fire and a body still strapped into a seat, hanging upside down from a nearby tree. She closed her eyes and let herself be led to a house across the street.

As is the case with most if not all air crashes, it was supposed to have been a routine voyage. Captain W.G. Foster checked his flight log as he and his copilot, C.E. Sinclair, waited for a young stewardess, Nancy Taylor, and her counterpart to finish assisting the passengers into their seats. Looking down at the clipboard in front of him, Foster noticed that the CAB had inspected his plane twice before getting a green light for takeoff. He understood what airport he was flying out of and agreed with the extra precaution. Back in the cabin, Miss Taylor walked up and down the aisle, checking if all the seatbelts were fastened and turning off the dome lights in favor of the low-glow ceiling nightlights. In her testimony to the Civil Aeronautics Board's investigators, she recalled the warming up of engines and taxiing altogether taking no more than five minutes.[156] When asked if anything seemed unusual, if there had been any sputtering or engine backfire, the young lady replied, "No, sir." Content with everything being secured, Nancy went to the back of the plane and strapped herself into her rear-facing seat. Foster began guiding his airplane off the Newark runway. It was just past midnight on February

11, 1952. With the plane still climbing, the young stewardess's head snapped to her right as she heard "a terrible noise." In her testimony, she stated, "As soon as I heard the noise, I knew we were going to crash, and I was facing the back end of the plane, and I couldn't see the engines. I stayed in my seat up until the time the aircraft crashed."

Taylor compared the noise to a firecracker. After further questioning, the young lady recalled that she first noticed the noise at about 700 or 1,000 feet. When asked how long after the noise the airplane crashed, the stewardess answered, "About a minute and a half…[the crew] did not have a chance to turn the plane around. It looked like it was coming straight in….I was looking at a lady with her baby in her arms and then 'poof.'"[157] Just seconds after engine failure and with the plane having climbed to 1,500 feet, the second engine imploded. Captain Foster knew that the likelihood of him making it back to the runway was very slim, but that would not prevent him from trying to save as many lives as possible. After messaging the tower that two of his engines had failed and being told to return to the field, he radioed in, "Can't make it!" They were his last words. The only thing left for him to do was fight to keep his out-of-control plane away from residential Elizabeth. Veering off toward the marshes, "the plane plunged into the crowded city like a guided bomb—just two minutes after it left the airport."[158] To lighten his load, Foster began to dump his fuel, which sprayed buildings below, making the fire that eventually ensued that much more difficult to contain.

The airliner was reported to have knifed through the top floor of a four-story brick apartment house, "wiping out one whole family of three." Another resident met his end on the second floor, "screaming behind a wall of flames."[159] The plane then struck and ricocheted off a building, throwing pieces of wreckage hundreds of yards around the perimeter. Amazingly, the craft broke into two parts, saving the lives of Nancy Taylor and thirty-four passengers in its tail section. While that part of the plane initially settled in a treetop, it quickly crashed to the street below, landing upside down. The second part, the front of the fuselage, catapulted into the playground of a children's home, burning fiercely.[160] Herman S. Goldford, the occupant of the building at the intersection of Salem Road and Westminster Avenue, where the plane crashed, stated, "The house shook…my wife and I got up and grabbed the children and ran, trying to get away. We [just] kept running, trying to get away from the searing heat."[161] Plane seats were scattered all over the city block. "There were pieces of plane all over the place," said Louis Ehrenberg, forty-five, a local resident. "I saw a man and pulled him out. He was dead. We pulled out

Elizabeth firemen attempt a rescue after the third plane, a National Airlines DC-6, crashed into a four-story apartment building. *Courtesy of Newark Public Library.*

more people—most of them dying. I picked up one man's arm, and it came away from his body. My son picked up a baby. It was dead too."[162] The nearby building, shaken by the impact and now aflame, came alive. Windows shattered, and doors burst opened as the residents of the lower floors stormed out of the front doors with babies and pets in their arms.[163]

The aftermath of the third crash, which saw the plane come down in the front yard of a local orphanage and school. The boys from the orphanage assisted in the rescue efforts. *Courtesy of Newark Public Library.*

Small explosions continued to rock the area. Kids at the Janet Memorial Home, an institution for children of broken homes barely missed by the crash, came out to the wreckage in their front lawn and began the rescue efforts as police and firemen sped to the scene. While the plane kept on exploding and burning for an hour after the crash, rescue workers and volunteers "couldn't get into the [dismembered] front section, but they did pick up persons who were laying within arm's length of that burning torch," said Mr. Goldstein, who lived in the Veteran's Apartment nearby. "Some persons walked away from that wreck, but how they did it, I'll never know."[164] The place was crowded with people. Bodies seemed to be spread out everywhere. The older children from the orphanage and first responders carried the injured and the dead across the street and laid them on the lawns. "The place was jammed with people. Most of them had bathrobes thrown over their pajamas," added Goldstein. "One man told me that he had just driven through Salem Road when the plane hit the building. The driver said that if the plane had been a little lower, it would have hit him."[165] Faces of

The February 11 crash. The picture showcases the rescue efforts near the back portion of the fuselage. *Courtesy of Newark Public Library.*

all those present were blank with shock, their bodies shivering in the cold and wet night. "At the orphanage, practically every window had youngsters, their faces pressed against the glass, peering out at the blazing plane."[166] It was recalled that everyone seemed to be in a daze. There was a strange quiet as the survivors climbed out of the broken-off rear section.

"She was a little girl, almost a baby. She had on a yellow hood. I couldn't leave her in there to burn. I couldn't do it," said patrolman Patrick Maloney.[167] One of the first on the scene, the officer was ordered to pull only the living out of the wreckage and leave behind those beyond any help. He knew that the little girl was no longer alive, but he also knew that he could not live with himself if he left her body to burn in the blazing wreckage. A short while after Maloney's conscience got the better of him, Robert English, who lived across the street from the crash, was standing at his window in disbelief, looking down at the commotion: "I couldn't see anything clearly—not the plane or anything else. Then, someone rang my doorbell. It was a man from the plane—splashed with blood from cuts on his head and hands. He asked me in a thick, faltering voice whether he could use the phone, but he couldn't get through to wherever he was trying to call."[168]

Bodies were being laid out in the playground before being carried across the street, and aluminum plane parts intertwined with the monkey bars and swing sets. In the building overlooking the bloodshed, a small group of the youngest children of the orphanage was led to the dining room by their supervisors for a glass of milk—anything to spare them witnessing—and never forgetting—the carnage outside.

The scene of terror in the already traumatized city was only three-quarters of a mile from the site of the December 16 crash of the non-scheduled C-46 that cost fifty-six lives. It was also just a little over a mile from the site of the January 22 crash of an American Airlines Convair that killed thirty more, including seven on the ground. A total of four occupants of the building that was struck, twenty-six of the plane's fifty-nine passengers and three of its four crew members were killed, with countless others suffering injuries. While death is part of the norm for any funeral home, Alfred C. Haines's business was far from the standard in the past fifty-eight days. The latest crash happened just around the block from Haines Funeral Home. As with prior accidents, the bodies of the twenty-nine victims were once again laid out in the garage behind the main structure. They lay on the cold concrete floor, "wrapped individually in blankets to which were attached any identifying items found."[169] The blankets covered everything but the feet of the victims—most of them were shoeless, as the crash had knocked them off. Shortly after 8:30 a.m., the first relatives of those killed in the disaster began to arrive to make the required identifications. Police officers held them back until they could confirm their own identities as to keep out any gawkers or reporters attempting to get inside. There were countless Red Cross workers assisting the police through the entire process. "We are getting to be old hands at this," said one police officer sadly.[170] Across the street, kids off school for President's Day arrived in droves. They carried small cameras on their way to capture shots of the wreckage right down the street.

In a press conference called by the airline, Captain Eddie Rickenbacker, president of the Eastern Air Lines, proclaimed that Newark was "a preferred airport" to pilots under any weather conditions. He added that in most pilots' opinion, "it is the best situated, best equipped, and the safest airport in the entire county."[171] While pilots representing five various airlines confirmed Rickenbacker's assertion, the figures and glorified talk had little effect on the people of Elizabeth. As they gathered outside the wreckage in the early morning hours, one man was heard shouting, "This is the last straw; how

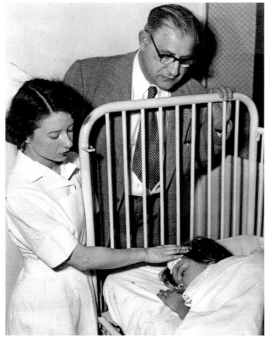

Above: The aftermath of the third crash. The front portion of the plane is seen smoldering. There were small explosions reported to have come out of the wreckage for a full hour after it had crashed. *Courtesy of Newark Public Library.*

Left: Patricia Clausen, five years of age and a passenger on the February 11, 1952 crash, is being cared for by a doctor and a nurse at the Elizabeth General Hospital. Her mother did not survive the crash. *Courtesy of Newark Public Library.*

A newspaper diagram detailing the three airplane crashes. The label of "Umbrella of Death" is first seen in the original description. *From* The Record, *February 11, 1964.*

much more can we take?"[172] At a hastily called special press conference, only hours after the fatal plane crash, New Jersey governor Alfred E. Driscoll answered the man by announcing his orders to close Newark Airport without waiting for legal action from the federal government. After ordering the attorney general to begin an immediate investigation of the tragedy, the visibly shaken governor stated that he had spoken to the Port Authority of New York representatives. He made it very clear that the latter was very supportive of his decision to close its airport, saying that they all felt "that irrespective of the law on the subject, the airport should be closed and the use of the runways terminated pending a thorough and complete investigation."[173] The order stated that the governor's intention was to at once terminate airplane flights over the congested areas of Elizabeth, Newark and neighboring communities. In his view, the airport could not reopen until changes were made to alter its flight patterns. Others, however, felt a bit stronger about the airfield's future, as was the case with New Jersey Representative Gordon Canfield. "In my opinion, the present Newark Airport is dead. Its awful dangers have been most tragically exposed, and it is so placed it will not lend itself to necessary future expansion."[174]

All takeoffs and landings scheduled for Newark Airport were transferred to LaGuardia Airport and New York (Idlewild) Airport, respectively. This sparked a new call by irate residents, this time those of Queens. The people living near LaGuardia Airport used local newspapers to demand the removal of the airport—"before," as one Queens leader put it, "there is a murder here."[175] A representative of the Eastern Queens Civic Council stated, "We heard today of the third murder in Elizabeth, NJ. This must not happen in Queens…[the airport] must be moved elsewhere." When

The map rendering shows the proximity of the three crashes to one another as well as to Newark Airport. *From the* Central New Jersey Home News *(New Brunswick). February 11, 1952.*

asked where he thought the field should move, he noted that it was not his concern. "We just don't want it in Queens!"[176] Other Queens residents sent telegrams to Austin J. Tobin, the Port Authority of New York director, asking for the immediate closing of the specific runway at LaGuardia. Their fears were not necessarily unwarranted. Just a few months later, an airplane crash in Queens would take the lives of five individuals when it came tumbling down on the crowded Jamaica neighborhood. The proponents of removing the Queens airport were met with the same obstacles as their New Jersey neighbors of Elizabeth. And just like them, their wishes would not be granted. It did not help that even after the second crash in Elizabeth, the Civil Aeronautics Administration's probes and investigations "proved" that "the three metropolitan area airports [including Newark and LaGuardia], fully meet the CAA regulations and the safety criteria developed by the CAA for the safeguarding of aircraft landing or taking off under instrument conditions."[177]

A state legislative committee tasked with the investigation of the three airline disasters promised that "blame [would] be placed where blame [was] due without hesitation, stay or whitewash."[178] Yet federal government and airline officials' probes and investigations at no point discussed keeping Newark Airport closed forever—no matter how much the state and local officials would have wanted them to. Meetings were regularly held by the port authority to discuss establishing new safety measures. They were attended by representatives of twenty-five domestic airlines, three transport associations, pilots, the Civil Aeronautics Administration and the Civil Aeronautics Board. The investigations into the latest crash and the overall safety of Newark Airport continued for days and weeks. Meanwhile, the CAA and the newly appointed fifteen-member Airline Committee, with American World War I ace Eddie Rickenbacker at its helm, met with the Air Transport Association's representatives to work out new flight schedules for LaGuardia, Idlewild and Teterboro Airports. The CAA, which operated airport towers, gave priority to the named airports, as they had now absorbed Newark's traffic after the latest crash. New regulations would "permit take-offs over water or over the sparsely settled areas as a matter of choice," adding that runways requiring flights over congested areas would be assigned "only when such use was mandatory for reasons of safety."[179]

Meanwhile, the six-member state legislative committee continued their hearings and probes into the disaster. During a February 21 meeting, public officials, including five mayors, and a slew of witnesses to the latest disaster testified for two hours in a closed-door meeting. William Runyon, Elizabeth

An investigator examines the carnage left behind the last of the three airplane crashes. *Courtesy of Newark Public Library.*

Board of Works commissioner, said it bluntly: "We want the airport taken away bag and baggage. If officials could see the results of the three crashes, they would be horrified. If we ever had a fourth crash in Elizabeth—God help Washington."[180] Joining Runyon were representatives from eight different municipalities located near the airport. Suggestions ranged from total removal of the airport—which was believed to have outgrown itself—to some outlying section to constructing emergency fields about five miles away from it to be used for emergency landings.[181] Charles Handler, Newark Corporation counsel, called for the state legislature to have the authorization to enact laws controlling the flights at Newark Airport. "Despite the authority vested in the Port Authority of New York, I do not believe the state can surrender its police powers of protecting the health and welfare of people living in the airport area," he stated.[182]

As the committee called for additional public hearings, President Truman appointed a special commission to investigate air crashes as well as the crowded and densely populated areas near airfields. A New Jersey senator stationed in Washington, D.C., H. Alexander Smith, presented to Congress and the media the outcome of the presidential commission. The news could not have been any worse for the people of Elizabeth. Namely, the state's politician acknowledged that Newark Airport would have to eventually be reopened, as there was simply no other place nearby to divert its heavy traffic.[183] Moreover, its otherwise clean bill of health and safety would only further warrant such a conclusion. Speaking publicly weeks after the February crash, Port Authority commissioner John F. Sly admitted that planes would probably never again be permitted to take off from Newark Airport on Runway 6-24, which was directed toward the heart of Elizabeth. Yet he provided a glimpse into what those calling for a total closure of the airport could expect. Namely, he informed the public that construction crews received no word to stop working on a new runway, regardless of the airport's current "closed" status. In case someone did not understand what he was alluding to, Sly and other port authority officials candidly stated that they assumed the airport would eventually reopen with a revamped safety code. Thus, many fought bitterly to stop what others already knew to be inevitable.

With the file closed and the airport's future in the air, all anxiously awaited the results of the investigations into the latest disaster; some hoped that it signaled some wrongdoing on the part of Newark Airport itself. In an editorial, the *Bergen Evening Record*'s chief editor penned the following on the day of the crash, mere hours after it had occurred, when the airfield's traffic was already shut down:

> *Only in blind and reckless folly could the Elizabeth plane disasters be depreciated as mere (however unfortunate) variations from a norm. It is good to see that in responsible places there is no disposition to deprecate*

them. Although it is not in control of air traffic at Newark Airport—that is the responsibility of the Civil Aeronautics Administration, the federal operating agency—the Port Authority of New York has used its physical possession of the port boldly and wisely to shut it down, at least pending investigation and the establishment of a pattern that doesn't involve periodic visitations of sudden and frightful death.

This third time engine failure seems to have caused a plane to falter in take-off and pancake into Elizabeth. To some rudimentary extent, then, No. 3 is like No. 1, in which apparently an engine took fire and the flame ate away the wing of a plane taking off. No. 2 was, of course, much different technically: an incoming plane fell off the ground beam…and topple[d] into the city.

These aberrations have just one thing in common: they acquired their full deadliness because Newark Airport and Elizabeth are hard against each other. This is not to say the accidents wouldn't have happened if the two were separated by a cordon of marsh or water 10 miles wide; but it is to point out that the essential diagnostic factor is the city's being where airplanes in trouble also are.

Well, we can't move Elizabeth, and it would be impossible to move Newark Airport without making something else, without creating new problems by abandoning our concern over and our efforts to solve present problems. The Port Authority's suspension of all flying at Newark does not solve these; but it creates an atmosphere in which solution becomes possible, and at the very least shatters the baleful pattern.

The narrative presented by the *Bergen Evening Record* showcased a different perspective. It turned the events away from an emotional issue of good versus evil and into one of logical debate. Without assigning any specific blame to the "evil" port authority or the CAA, the editor took the time to commend the right response taken by both after the terrific accidents in Elizabeth. It also hoped that those involved who had the power to bring about changes were indeed willing to do what was needed to ensure everyone's safety—and, perhaps more importantly, to do so for the right reasons and not because of emotional outbursts. To the dismay of many—and as initially suspected—the third crash, as with the first two, was proven to be of no fault on the part of Newark Airport, the port authority or the CAA. What was needed now was not assigning further blame but rather coming up with appropriate measures and safeguards to do the inevitable effectively: open the once largest national airport. As is often the case with history, we may know the end result, but we

An area of the third airplane crash being guarded by Elizabeth police. *From the* Central New Jersey Home News *(New Brunswick). February 11, 1952.*

are oblivious to the process and journey toward its realization. And in this case, the fight for (and against) Newark Airport was far from over.

When it was all said and done, the CAB File No. 1 10015 outlined the probable cause of the crash as "the reversal in the flight of no. 3 propeller with relatively high power and the subsequent feathering of no. 4 propeller resulting in a descent at an altitude too low to effect recovery."[184] The CAA was quick in addressing the issue, as was outlined in its philosophy statement, to minimize the possibility of it ever happening again. The probable cause of the propeller reversal brought about an order to the airlines and the aircraft industry for a safer shielding and isolation of the wiring system that controlled the reversing gear on all craft similar to the plane that had been destroyed.[185] Yet none of this mattered to those who wholeheartedly opposed the continued existence of the airport itself. According to Knight, in his study of airplane disasters published in 1958, the major issue about whether Newark Airport could ever reopen dealt with what changes and protections it could and would implement (as well as guarantee) to quell the fears of Elizabeth's population, tired of living under "an umbrella of death."

Chapter 6

A BATTLE FOR THE FATE OF AN AIRPORT

W ith another group of people being laid to rest and the airport's future very much still in the air, the site of Newark Airport itself was full of noise. Without any flight interruption, the port authority, as it awaited its fate from the CAA and the CAB as well as the federal government, sped up its efforts to construct a new seven-thousand-foot instrument runway along with a new terminal. In an editorial from the *Hackensack Record*, Fred L. Wehran, former owner and operator of Teterboro Airport, now the biggest air terminal in the east, defended the port authority's actions. "Newark Airport operated for more than 20 long years without one really tragic crash. Think of the thousands of flights in and out of this great airport under all weather conditions without a single serious mishap which certainly dramatized the recent three highly spectacular accidents that may not be duplicated in many further years of operations....Surely, it should not be condemned to death without a chance to resurrect itself."[186] After selling his airport for a large sum of money to the very same port authority he was now defending, the "expert" stated, "[C]ertainly, I deeply sympathize with the victims of the tragedies and the people of Elizabeth and fully agree with them that their lives and property should not be further jeopardized." Adding that the accidents were due to mechanical and weather-related incidents, and thus were not the fault of the airport, Wehran reasserted that such accidents as occurred in Elizabeth could and would be avoided by changing flying patterns and constructing runways that moved the planes' departures and arrivals away from congested areas. With that in mind, Newark Airport's

Newark Airport Now Ghost Field, Its Future In Balance

The future of Newark Airport was up in the air within days of the third crash. *From the* Daily Press, *February 12, 1952.*

newest endeavor to build a new and much longer instrument runway was right on point and the best response the port authority could have had to the terrible tragedies. The new runway, 4R-22L, led out toward open water and the uninhabited marshy fingers of the bay shore. Most importantly, when finished, it would lead directly away from the city of Elizabeth.[187] Its completion was mere months away. Meanwhile, the battle for Newark Airport raged on the streets of Elizabeth, in local and national newspapers and behind closed doors at Congressional hearings, where men and women of various agencies bitterly fought for and against the airport.

The seemingly undisputed belief that the third crash marked the end of Newark Airport made it that much more of a surprise when Secretary of Commerce Charles Sawyer went on the record just a few days after its closure, saying that he expected its reopening "on a restricted basis" sooner rather than later.[188] Speaking at Florida State University, Mr. Sawyer also stated that the three Elizabeth accidents were due only to coincidence. And while the secretary understood the alarm felt by Elizabeth residents who demanded that the airport be closed, he also wanted them to know that the port authority was near completion on the much-needed runway that would eliminate all threats of further crashes into the center of the city. With the public outcry to Sawyer's statement visible through the editorial pages of local newspapers, the port authority made it very clear that it was "in no way responsible for Mr. Sawyer's statement and had nothing whatsoever to do with it," as stated by Austin J. Tobin, executive director of the port authority. The public outcry was very much against the port authority, and while even at that time it was not given any indication that it would be forced to close its doors forever, revealing such information in a delicate climate directly after the third crash would not have been wise. Thus, while the Congressional investigation by the special House subcommittee continued its hearings throughout February and March 1952, Mr. Tobin, Commissioner John F. Sly and Aviation Director Fred M. Glass were more than cooperative with the inquiry, trying to keep secret the fact that their airport would in all probability reopen.

To the dismay of those living in Elizabeth, Newark or near any other major airport throughout the nation, the investigation proved what many were already thinking. Namely, that Newark Airport's CAA label as one of the safest if not *the* safest airport in the nation was closer to the truth than the three tragedies would indicate. The only real attack that could have been pointed at the airfield was at one of its outdated runways, no. 10. According to testimonies, the older runway was rejected by the pilot of the third plane on February 11 due to being defective and full of "small ripples" in its pavement. This was significant, as runway no. 10 pointed over Newark Bay instead of the crowded Elizabeth, which the pilot instead chose to go over by taking runway no. 24. In denying that runway no. 10 was defective, Mr. Glass insisted that fifty planes had used that runway the morning of the crash to fly to other airfields when the shutdown was announced—thus, it was a matter of individual pilot preference that led to the use of runway no. 24 pointing toward Elizabeth and not any real fault with runway no. 10.[189] After investigators examined the airfield in question, while admitting that it was in need of being replaced soon— something that was already in motion before the second and third crash with the construction of the new instrument runway—they backed the aviation director's claims that it was more than suitable for operation on that fateful day. As it began to seem more likely there would once again not be any fault found on the part of the port authority or Newark Airport, much work still needed to be done to convince the people of Elizabeth and Newark that it was safe for the airport to reopen.

What is often not considered when examining the fate of Newark Airport during those fateful months following the three air disasters was its military role. When it was forced to shut down, the U.S. military had already made the New Jersey airport the main hub of operations in shipping planes overseas to General Eisenhower's North Atlantic Treaty Organization forces. This point was overlooked by the population at the time yet needs to be addressed as perhaps the biggest factor in reopening the airport. When viewed in the context of homeland security—which many people's emotions prohibited them from doing directly after the crashes—the reopening of the closed airfields should always have been one of "when" and not "if." Biding its time as not to stir up too much resentment, as well as to pay its respects to the families of those affected by the disasters, the U.S. Air Force temporarily moved its operations to the small (and inadequate for the purpose) Floyd Bennett Field in Brooklyn, New York. When it was becoming clear by late March 1952 that Newark Airport could not be blamed for the disasters, and with the construction of the new field in full swing, Newark's Mayor Ralph Villani held a behind-closed-doors-meeting with the air force's Assistant Secretary Edwin V. Huggins. For those following the news in the papers, albeit tucked away within them as opposed to glaring at readers from their front pages, they would not be surprised such a meeting was taking place. The air force was very vocal about explaining Newark Airport's role in dismantling military planes flown in and then crated for water shipments for NATO—the fact that not many people were aware of prior to this time. In their defense, the military alliance had only been around for less than three years. Regardless, the shutdown had placed U.S. security in jeopardy and those of its allied nations in the fight against Communism in Europe.

By March 19, the *Courier News* of Bridgewater, New Jersey, was reporting on the now not-so-secret meeting explaining the military's concern over the airport's closure significantly slowing down shipments of planes to Western European nations.[190] With the initial meeting procuring a follow-up, this time with Elizabeth's Mayor Kirk and State Senator Kenneth C. Hand of Union present, news began to come out that the airport would indeed be opening back up on a limited basis, though strictly for military purposes. The air force spokesman was quoted in the papers reassuring the people of nearby Elizabeth and Newark that if the airport were allowed to reopen on a limited basis—which would be essential to national security—flights would be limited to only incoming military planes, which would be processed for overseas shipment. The spokesman also added that "all planes would avoid flying over residential areas and land only in good weather with favorable winds."[191] In responding to the rumors, Senator Hand attempted to keep some hope alive for his county and state constituents, as well as those concerned citizens of the affected city. The senator, who also happened to be the head of the newly established Mayor's Committee for Air Safety, stated that he "[could] find no quarrel if [the air force were] going to use the field for necessary military operations." However, he quickly added that he hoped that "the action was not part of a long-range plan to open the airport a few weeks for military flights and then throw it open for all commercial flights."[192]

The context of the time comes in very handy when attempting to understand the impetus for people's wholehearted support of reopening the airport for military use. In 1952, the United States was enduring Senator McCarthy's Communist witch hunt. It was barely a year removed from the executions of Julius and Ethel Rosenberg for passing atomic secrets to the Soviets. And the overall fear of the growing threat with China falling to Communism and now fighting against U.S. forces alongside North Korea made national security a priority for many. Subsequently, "patriotism" and the duty to one's nation overpowered the bottled-up rage, fear and resentment against Newark Airport. Although not a full reopening by any means, allowing the usage of Newark Airport by the air force permitted enough time to pass to finish the construction of the new instrument airfield and hence take away any argument the people of Elizabeth or Newark still had against the airport's unsafe flying patterns. "This approval shows, we think, that the attitude of the suburban areas has not been unreasonable," stated one editorial. "They are willing to subject themselves to the risks of living near an airport for patriotic reasons; they are not willing to subject themselves to such risks for the private profit of others....The nation's need should prevail."[193] Despite Senator Hand's and Mayor Kirk's assurances of the airport not opening for commercial flights, it took hardly another three months for the first commercial planes to once again begin landing on Newark Airport's airfields—despite rounds of protests from civil groups that did everything in their power to keep the field closed for good.

Riding on the patriotic coattails of opening the metropolitan airport to the military, the port authority's real goal of a full reopening got a major boost from two of the most nationally recognized and revered aviation celebrities of the time. Speaking at a luncheon before the Newark Chamber of Commerce on April 16, 1952, Captain Eddie Rickenbacker, the president of Eastern Air Lines and an American fighter ace pilot from World War I as well as a Medal of Honor recipient, stated, "There can be no disputing the fact that...Newark Airport should be reopened at once."[194] This time around, it was not patriotism that was driving the full reopening of the airport, but rather the one thing that would appeal to all: economy and jobs. Rickenbacker said that he spoke to the National Air Transport Coordinating Committee, which was formed hours after the third Elizabeth plane crash, and requested to "combine the voluntary efforts of all elements of civil aviation, toward the earliest possible solution to the critical problems... involving Newark Airport."[195] The World War I ace once again pointed to the airport's perfect safety record in the two decades before what he called an "unprecedented combination of circumstances." Yet the biggest weapon up his sleeve was the appeal to the people of Elizabeth and Newark to consider the effect a long-term closing of the airfields would have on their livelihoods. In a detailed fifteen-page statement full of statistics, the one-time pilot explained Newark Airport's vital role in the Newark/New York City area's economy and New Jersey as a whole. Based on his numbers, he stated that the impact of the airport's closing "threw thousands of [local] persons out of work."[196]

One month later, the famed airman once again publicly pleaded to reopen Newark Airport, even before the completion of the new instrument runway. Citing the need to save local jobs and businesses as quickly as possible, Rickenbacker outlined an eight-point safety program of the "most far-reaching adjustment of operational procedures ever undertaken by the industry"—one that was designed to "improve public safeguards and reduce noise" at the three major airports in the metropolitan area, including Newark.[197] The program, whose specifics were not made public at the time, was devised through the voluntary cooperation of the CAA, air carriers, private aircraft and airport operators and airline pilots. According to the national aviation celebrity, the new program was justification enough to help the needy people of the area who had lost their jobs as a result of the airport's closing. Not downplaying the fears and concerns of those living in Elizabeth and Newark, the ace reassured them that if the airport were opened immediately, flight activity as specified in the new safety program would be 50 percent less than the normal pre-closing amount. He added that the proper number of flights would be reached only when the new runway was completed in November.[198]

The November date that Rickenbacker kept referring to was November 1, 1952. It was the day that was publicly announced by the port authority on May 11 as the official date of the airport's reopening. And just as it was expected, the opposition to the first concrete news of a reopening plan was instantaneous. Voicing their opinions within days, those present at the meeting of the Mayor's Committee in Elizabeth—composed of representatives from communities in the Newark-Elizabeth area—compelled the group to authorize a resolution opposing the reopening. The impetus rested on the claim that the various investigations into the crashes had not yet been completed. The resolution, drawn up by State Senator Kenneth Hand, was sent to New Jersey governor Driscoll, Congress and the port authority.[199] As to the claims that the new runway would solve all of the problems by diverting flights away from Elizabeth and Newark, Councilman William J. Hurst of the nearby town of Linden (and a representative of the committee) told the group that a new runway was being built at Newark

Airport would aim planes over the giant oil refineries and chemical plants in his city, once more presenting a threat of "greater disaster."[200] Voicing his displeasure to the new announcement and reopening date was Newark city commissioner Meyer C. Ellenstein. The statesman openly doubted that the new runway would solve any of the safety and noise problems. Meanwhile, Senator Hand publicly stated that the announcement "indicates to me that the Port Authority plans to reopen Newark Airport on a grand scale, larger even than it was before." He added, "This is bad news for the people of this area....I am disappointed that Governor Driscoll did not comply with our request that he veto this huge building project."[201]

Further arguing against a full reopening of Newark Airport, Ellenstein gave an interview to the Associated Press in which he went on record saying that the new runway would not solve the problems of safety and noise, and he believed that approving it was nothing short of falling for the port authority's veil of deception. "The Port Authority doesn't control the winds," he said. "Airplanes must take off against the wind. If the wind is in the wrong direction, they'll have to use another runway. That other runway will be the new east–west runway when it is completed." Pointing to the map at one of the new runways being built, the commissioner stated, "It will send planes flying over Newark's densely populated Clinton Hill residential section."[202] The main instrument runway that was being finished by November and hyped as the saving grace of the airport was a north–south runway. Ellenstein pointed to another, smaller east–west airstrip that was also being constructed concurrently with the larger one. Interestingly enough, even with an established reopening date, the CAA was still actively seeking a location for a new metropolitan airport to accommodate the tri-state area. It was perhaps the failure of securing an appropriate place and the influx of petitions against it from the towns of potential sites that strengthened the CAA's resolve to continue its support for the full reopening of Newark Airport. The most notable example was Parsippany, New Jersey, designated as the best suited for a new international airport. Yet, as was suspected, the rebuttal from the township committee was instantaneous. Dudley Kimball, chairman of the Parsippany–Troy Hills Township, publicly stated that his municipality was never consulted by the CAA on the proposal and said it would oppose its use completely. Citing the three Elizabeth tragedies, Kimball pointed out that the proposed airport would physically split the township, which he said was a class-A residential community that was densely populated.[203] And so, the CAA went back to favoring Newark Airport, especially with all the changes proposed for its reopening in November of that year.

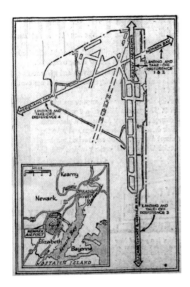

Press release of the new airfield on the eve of the reopening of Newark Airport, showing the closed, ill-fated airstrip (*middle of image*). *From the* Belleville Times, *November 13, 1952.*

As the Mayor's Committee awaited its answer from the governor, another aviation celebrity threw his support behind the port authority and the airport's reopening. At a press conference on May 16, 1952, James H. Doolittle, chairman of the federal Airport Commission created by President Truman following the Elizabeth crashes, went public with his expert opinion that Newark Airport was safe and needed to be reopened. The world-famous flyer and World War II hero made the statement after handing President Truman a two-hundred-page report containing scores of recommendations as to the location and use of the nation's airports. Pressed by reporters for more information, Doolittle said that he would "climb way out on a limb" and say that "Newark Airport, measured by standards that indicate the safety or lack of safety of other airports, is a safe airport."[204]

He added that any safe airport should be used because "we need more and better airports." The famed flyer also admitted that he was not permitted to single out any fields for being safer than others. Furthermore, he verbalized what many already knew but fought against regardless: namely, that not too much could be done to make airports less noisy. With the federal commission giving its blessing and the CAA and CAB's investigations giving the thumbs up to the improved safety measures at the airport, and with no fault found on the part of the airport in the five separate probes into the latest airplane crash, the fate of Elizabeth and Newark was sealed.

Chapter 7

BACK TO THE NEW NORMAL

Fred Gross of Stelton checked the gauges of his Beechcraft Bonanza six-seater, single-engine aircraft. His beloved wife, Jane, and Mrs. Frederick Osman of Stelton were sitting beside him and directly behind. Fred felt very comfortable behind the controls of the small Appointment Airways airplane. He was one of the most experienced New York company's air-taxi pilots. It was a Saturday, November 11, 1952, nearly a year from the first and about nine months since the last airplane crash in Elizabeth, New Jersey. Fred adjusted his plane for an approach from the south, over the Newark meadows. Everything went as it should have as the small aircraft touched down on a brand-new runway at 12:05 a.m. With it, Fred's plane became the first to officially land at Newark Airport as it resumed its full operations after a nine-month curtailment brought on by the three tragedies.[205] The new runway 4R-22L was equipped with new avionics, radar and lighting equipment—all installed to improve the safety of landings and takeoffs, at a cost to the port authority of about $9 million.[206] As his plane taxied toward the terminal, Mr. Gross did not pay any notice to the darkness west of him and his aircraft. Perhaps if he stopped and really strained his eyes, he might have even seen it. Directly below the night sky, illuminated strictly by the stars in the heavens and lacking any artificial lighting, lay the remnants of runway 6-24, never to be used again. The Newark Airport was officially back open for business.

WHEN ON JUNE 19 the Port Authority of New York voted 11-0 for reopening the airport ahead of schedule, for limited service in a few days' time and eventually to full service in November of that year, two children who were injured in one of the crashes were still in the hospital. Despite new restrictions guiding the airport's operations, the initially limited number of flights and even the eventual opening of a new runway toward the end of the year, the residents of Elizabeth could not believe the events unfolding in front of them. Fifty-eight days, three airplane crashes and 119 people dead, 11 of whom lived in the city—and just like that, Newark Airport was reopening once more. To them, their politicians, their local and federal government and, in some sense, the world had failed them. "We regret very much the fact that the authority did not give much weight to our opposition," said Kenneth C. Hand, the head of the Mayor's Committee and an Elizabeth resident.[207] The Associated Press printed the assurances of Howard S. Cullman of the port authority, stating that all the new restrictions followed precisely those recommendations by a National Transport Coordinating Committee, which was organized after the three crashes. Statements reaffirming Newark Airport's safety had also been issued by both the Civil Aeronautics Administrator and General James Doolittle, chairman of a presidential Commission on National Airport Policy.[208] For the people of Elizabeth and Newark and Newark Airport's stakeholders, it would be the beginning of a new normal. And so, when the port authority dedicated its new $8.5 million terminal on July 29, 1953, and Doolittle once more assured the crowd gathered at Newark Airport that they were standing "in one of the best and safest airports in the world," conspicuously absent from the crowd were the mayors of all adjacent towns.[209]

As Newark Airport opened for limited service, mostly cargo and shipment flights, with commercial airliners not coming back until November, it had indeed done so with important changes to its safety protocols. Apart from the aforementioned new landing strip, the National Transport Coordinating Committee set forth three main restrictions in order to protect the residents of nearby Elizabeth and Newark. There would be no takeoffs from runways leading over Newark and Elizabeth, no landings from the direction of Elizabeth and no instrument landings on the outdated airstrip. Operations were only permitted when there was a minimum ceiling of one thousand feet and three miles visibility.[210] When the news broke of the airport's ahead-of-schedule (albeit limited) opening, Charles Handler of the Mayor's Committee proclaimed that they would once again try to get an injunction in Superior Court to

One of the hangars at Newark Airport around the time of the crashes. *Courtesy of Newark Public Library.*

stop the authority's operation of the airport. But even with newspapers reporting that many residents were threatening to "move out of town," it was generally agreed that such an injunction was too little and too late, as it could not be obtained in time to stop the opening of the airport. To calm some of the residents' nerves, the CAA announced that "any pilot or operator who did not comply with the restrictions set down by the authority would have enforcement actions initiated against him."[211]

Ironically, within a week of reopening on a limited basis, an angry Union County prosecutor, one Edward Cohn, charged that he saw a low-flying airplane over Elizabeth. When he rushed to report it, he found the Civil Aeronautics Administration safety office at Newark Airport closed for the weekend. Feeling like he was not allowed to record the injunction, he went on record with a local paper, stating, "If this is the best they can offer in the way of safety, they themselves will have to close Newark Airport because of failure to provide adequate regulations."[212] Threatening to go to Washington to lodge a formal complaint with the CAA authorities, he told reporters, "This is a terrible disappointment after all the promises of strict enforcement made so readily by the CAA and others." As much as it would have made for a great narrative for those opposing the newly reopened airport, the CAA was able to confirm days later that no four-engine plane had taken off or landed at Newark that day, suggesting that the plane that Cohn saw may have been heading to or from LaGuardia or Idlewild Airports in New York.

Since its reopening, the airport had been operating under very strict regulations and limitations. On June 16, 1952, its official first day of limited-basis operation, Newark Airport welcomed 11 port authority employees back to work. And while by the end of the week the number had grown to 74, it was still short of the normal complement of 113.[213] "All we need now are customers," an authority spokesman stated in a media briefing. After spending the entire weekend leading up to the opening busing itself in and putting the airport back together, the port authority was indeed ready. As for the big airline business, that would still have to wait. Not wanting to stir up further opposition and resentment from residents of the area—which would be bad for future business and brand loyalty—the big airlines withheld their flights from Newark's airfields until the completion of the new instrument runway in November. Thus, June's soft opening was not necessarily what the airport owners hoped for. Still, for them, it was a step in the right direction. The Associated Press once again reported on the busy airport in the days leading to June 16.

> All signs reading "Field Closed" that some hoped would never come down, were replaced with place cards proclaiming, "Field is Open—Do Not Cross the Runways." In the terminal building, the candy stand stocked up on supplies. A squad of girls was preparing to give service at a snack bar. Telephone repairmen worked on installations in the airlines' offices. A loudspeaker was tested.[214]

Not far removed from the smiling faces of the returning employees, there was a constant reminder of the tragedies' past looming in plain sight. One could not miss the large red *X* painted at the end of the north–south runway to remind pilots that flights over the center of Elizabeth were banned.

When Fred Gross became the first official pilot of the first official plane to land at the new instrument runway that November, it was not lost on him what he was doing. As reported that day's newspaper editions, the pilot wanted to be the first one in and the first one out on the airport's new $9 million runway. "It's a great improvement," he told the reporters. "I could have landed at LaGuardia or other airports," said the pilot of the small four-person plane, "and I could have landed at Newark on another runway [open since June], but I stayed up there about 15 minutes until the new runway was officially opened."[215] Still, while safety experts proclaimed the long-closed airfield safe and operational, it appeared that major airlines were still in no hurry to return, even though the airport had been technically open for nearly five months. The new schedule in operation the first fully operational week in November called for only 102 flight movements a day, more than 60 percent of peak operations the airport had on the eve of the first crash a year prior.[216] And that is not to say that Newark Airport was fully ready to accept the returning business. A month after reopening, local papers were still full of advertisements seeking to fill vacant jobs. Squeezed between the headlines were glaring Newark ads: "Immediate openings at Newark Airport," "mechanics sought" and "radio operators wanted."[217]

Although it took a while, inevitably, the big airlines came back. The location, a mere fifteen minutes away from one of the largest metropolitan areas in the world; the modernization of the airfield into one technologically ahead of its counterparts by leaps and bounds; and the unavoidable desire of many to have access to swift air travel made it preordained. Two days after the complete reopening of the airfield, an editorial came out in Elizabeth's local paper. Reprinted in numerous papers around the state, it showed people coming to terms with the fact that the opening of Newark Airport was inescapable. It was simply part of the natural progression of society relying on technology and innovation, even if, in the case of air travel, this new comfort could pose a threat to life. At least some people were willing to take the risk:

> *Reopening of Newark Airport for unrestricted flight operations is good news for businessmen who use the airlines often and to infrequent travelers who found it inconvenient getting to and from LaGuardia Field while New Jersey's major airport was closed.*
>
> *Elizabeth's residents—shuddering at the memory of three tragic crashes within two months—have been assured that…no longer will low-flying transports glide in or fight for altitude over the center of Elizabeth. The new safety rules…suggest that Newark's field is as safe as any airport in the world can be. Accident statistics remind the air traveler that he's twice as safe aloft as he would be in his own car, no matter how cautiously he drives.*
>
> *That doesn't mean that another great transport, headed in or out, couldn't crash over New Jersey. It may never happen, but it could occur tomorrow. Mechanical trouble contributed to…the Elizabeth disasters. All we know is that 1) the mathematical chances of mishap are very slight and 2) safety measures have been stepped up considerably at Newark.*
>
> *With everything done that can be done, we who choose to live in this closely built up metropolitan area are not going to give up our means of*

swift transport because air travel means putting one's safety into the keeping of two men up forward in the pilot's compartment.

We've just been told of the destructive possibilities of a hydrogen bomb, which could devastate an area much larger than an A-Bomb could lay waste, and we know we're sitting in a nest of war industries, but nobody's heading for the hills.[218]

There is no indication of who wrote the editorial, but it would be hard to believe that an Elizabeth resident wrote it. For better or for worse, and if not exactly in those words, it simply called on the people to move on. There was no stopping progress.

In the end, apart from the reworked and updated Newark Airport, the CAB probe did bring about one additional rule change: a revision of a propeller reversal wiring on all DC-6's, ordered by the federal agency when it discovered that reversal of a propeller in flight was one contributing cause of the February 11, 1952 crash.[219] Planes continued to fly in and out of the airport. In July 1953, months after the reopening and nearly two years since the first crash, a new passenger terminal opened. For Newark Airport, there was no looking back; the only way to go was forward. The new North Terminal was handling more than 1.4 million people by 1964. Even by 1957, more than 2.5 million passengers went through the terminal, a big change from the mere 100,000 in 1935 when the first large terminal opened. In 1966, about 4.5 million passengers flew in and out of Newark Airport, making it one of the world's busiest terminals.[220] Examining data collected by the Flight Safety Foundation, the airport's record of accidents at or near Newark Airport since the third crash totals eighteen separate occurrences. The total possible casualties from these accidents would have amounted to a staggering 1,434 people—in reality, and for lack of a better word, "only" 2 had lost their lives. While the last occurrence happened in June 2019, it should be noted that the research excludes the 9/11 attacks and the Boeing plane that left from Newark Airport on that fateful day. With all data compiled, it becomes evident that the assurances given to the people of Elizabeth in 1952 were not without merit. There were only two mentioned deaths through the nearly twenty potential calamities when a night check courier flight of a small plane occupied by two people "descended steep and fast on a runway and bounced on landing. Both pilots were exposed to marijuana and CO_2 in their blood from smoking."[221]

As reported by the Associated Press on the one-year anniversary of the first crash, the Institute of Life Insurance in New York had estimated that insurance companies paid out $1,462,000 on 210 life insurance policies held by survivors of the victims of the three crashes.[222] According to the article, airlines paid out many more thousands of dollars in damage suits, some of which were still pending in courts a year after the crashes.

NEARLY FIFTY YEARS HAD passed since the trilogy of Elizabeth accidents when, in April 2000, the pilots of a Continental Airlines flight to Belgium, with 234 occupants on board, lined up their McDonnel Douglass DC-10-30 on runway 04L and applied takeoff power slowly and smoothly. Almost immediately after takeoff, there was a loud explosion, and a white "engine fail" light lit up the instrument panel in front of the captain. The no. 1 engine decreased by more than 30 percent. According to National Transportation Safety Board's accident investigation report, the captain continued with his takeoff and turned the now vibrating plane as he slowly climbed to three thousand feet.[223] While eerily similar circumstances brought down the aircraft on the homes of Elizabeth residents many years prior, the technological advancements in aircraft and flight, as well as new flight patterns and safety measures taken up at Newark Airport in the weeks, months and years following the three tragedies from the winter of 1951–52, ensured that there would not be a repeat of those three tragic days. Air-traffic control personnel "provided vectors for a return to Newark" that avoided having the airplane near any residential area during its descent.[224] After dumping about ninety thousand pounds of fuel, the captain flew the ILS guideship to a full stop, landing on runway 04R heading away from the busy streets of Elizabeth. It was 8:16 p.m. as the plane touched down, just minutes after it had taken off.[225] A few short miles away in Elizabeth, people were getting their children ready for bed. Safely tucked away with their teddies and blankets, the little ones slept under the stars and the quiet skies above.

EPILOGUE

While no history books have been written directly about the Elizabeth airplane tragedies, the events have popped up in various newspaper articles throughout the years. The two most notable works describing the plane crashes and their aftermath are Judy Blume's novel *In the Unlikely Event* and Judy L. Mandel's *New York Times* bestselling memoir, *Replacement Child*. Apart from the two books, to better understand the tragedy's impact, one would need to search through the editorials, articles and interviews that were printed in the years following the crashes. Doing so grants us the ability to examine the events once more—this time through the lens of time. It is impossible to read a book and understand its story by burying our face in it and placing our noses right into its pages. Yet as we move our face farther away from the book, the picture and the story become that much clearer. The same analogy can best be applied to understanding the terrible crashes that changed a city and an airport and the air industry as a whole. The events as transcribed in these pages mainly came from primary documents and interviews from the time they took place. To provide a proper end to the story of the Elizabeth tragedies, we must also look at how the events had been interpreted, digested and, one might say, accepted with the passage of time. As long as those affected by the tragedies live to share their stories, fully understanding the impact of the tragedies recounted within these pages will be analyzed and evaluated. Like the amazing works by Blume and Mandel, hopefully, this work will add to the recording and the preservation of the legacy of those whose lives were forever changed by the events of the winter of 1951–52.

In an interview for the local paper forty years after the events of the Elizabeth trilogy of terror, Ernest H. Finizio, who was eleven years old at the time, was still coming to terms with the most traumatizing event of his childhood. "I can remember my family taking me down to show me [the wreckage]," said Finizio, at the time of the interview a superintendent of schools in Roselle Park. "I remember a sense of intimidation and fear. I remember the talk of them wanting to move."[226] Using his position as an educator, Finizio, who believed that that the crashes should not have been buried in history, included discussions of air safety issues in lesson plans in his school district. In the same article, Union County undersheriff John J. Troiano, who was a police officer in nearby Linden at the time, spoke of his mind often taking him back to those days, forty years before. "Some things you [just] don't forget," he said. "This left an impression on everyone." Troiano was a young police officer when the second crash occurred on January 22, 1952. He had just returned home from working the day shift when, like many police and medical workers from nearby towns, he was immediately recalled to the crash site in Elizabeth. He had to do it all over again on February 11, 1952. All those years later, he could still recall the shock and disbelief of receiving that second phone call just a few weeks after the events of the second crash. George O'Leary of Tewksbury, who was an eight-year-old resident of Elizabeth during the tragedies, said that he would never live near an airport again. He remembered the smoldering rubble. "It was terrifying." Yet what was really stuck in the memory of the forty-seven-year-old man was the look on people's faces. "[They] were just shaking their heads…they just couldn't believe it."

As recently as 2018, Chuck O'Donnell of the *Union News Daily* conducted interviews with the survivors and longtime Elizabeth citizens for a commemoration of the crashes in September of that year. More than thirty individuals came together at the corner of Williamson and South Streets to recall their memories of the three crashes that took place in their hometown. Hosted by the owner of an ice cream shop that was built in 1954 on the very same corner that once held the remnants of the crashed plane, the event was highlighted by the mayor, who spoke of the legacy of the crashes and how even sixty-seven years later, they still reverberated through the town.[227] Standing in the crowd was *New York Times* bestselling author Judy Mandel. She was not there to sign autographs; in fact, it was only the second time in her life that she could bring herself to return to the place of a crash that killed her sister Donna and left another sister, Linda, badly burned. Miss Mandel was born after the crash in 1954. While conducting research for her memoir of the events that set the course for her own life, Mandel came across the term "replacement child," described by 1960s psychologists Albert and Barbara Cain as a child conceived shortly after parents have lost another child. It all seemed so clear to her. In the interview for the *Union News Daily*, the author explained how at that moment, she finally understood why her father had been distant and her mother so overprotective. "I can almost hear my mother telling me I should not be here," Mandel said. "I can hear her say, 'Why are you coming back here? I tried to get you out of here.' I mean, that's a strange thing to say, but I know it was a painful place." She added, "As that replacement, I was supposed to be away from it and protected from it and shielded from it. So, they didn't want me to be any part of it."[228]

Judy recalled how her father was at work when the plane crashed into their home at 3:45 p.m. Her mom, having been knocked to the floor by the large explosion and with flames and debris everywhere, guided her elderly mother to safety. She then returned to the building and found Donna's friend, Sheila, who was on fire. She quickly threw a rug around her and brought her outside. Florence Mandel then returned to the flaming building and found her elder daughter pinned to the floor under some debris. As she attempted to help her, the young girl yelled at her mother to get her baby sister first. The heroic mother scooped up her baby and ran out of the building. As Florence turned around to get back inside, she was grabbed by some bystanders and not allowed to return to the badly burning structure. While little popping explosions continued to come from the debris, Mrs. Mandel could still hear Donna calling for her. A moment later, the entire building collapsed, and the cries for help ceased forever. "My mom was a hero," Judy Mandel said in 2018. "She never spoke about it. I think she felt she didn't save her other daughter. She didn't save Donna. But we know if she had gone back into that building when she wanted to, I wouldn't be here. She wouldn't have made it. The floor collapsed right as she was trying to get back in. And they held her back."[229]

THE SUCCESS OF NEWARK airport seemed almost inevitable. While many spent months in the winter of 1951–52 and long after fighting for the airfields to remain closed forever, a *New York Times* editorial perhaps said it best. "It is not possible to remove landing fields to entirely uninhabited areas. To do so would destroy the very value of air transport; it is not possible."[230] In the end, it was because of the fact that Newark was so close to metropolitan areas, and not in spite of it, that its survival was ensured. The proximity to one of the largest cities in the world, a plethora of industries and being within the dead center of one of the most populated areas in the nation made its return to glory inevitable. Even unlikely disasters that impacted the lives of so many and terrified entire city populations living near airfields throughout the nation could not derail Newark Airport's revival.

Today, Newark Liberty Airport has three major terminals: A, B and C. The airport's name was changed to incorporate "Liberty" in memory of the events of September 11, 2001, referring to the landmark Statue of Liberty, slightly more than five miles away from the airport's airfields. According to the Port Authority of New York and New Jersey, the City of Newark invested more than $8.2 million, the U.S. government spent more than $15.1 million and the port authority itself invested more than $4.3 billion to build and develop the airport.[231] About twenty thousand people are employed at Newark Liberty, and the airport contributes about $22.9 billion in economic activity to the New York/New Jersey metropolitan area. Furthermore, the airport also leads to about 162,000 jobs and $8.3 billion in annual salaries in the region. In 2008, the airport's number of flights was restricted to eighty-one per hour to soothe the air congestion near its metropolitan areas. It is considered one of the most modern, busiest and safest airports in the nation. Like everything else, though, Newark Airport has a story. In this case, it is one of pain, loss and, ultimately, redemption.

NOTES

Introduction

1. John Pelletreau, "Pilot Lived Three Blocks from Crash Scene; Wife Had Premonition as She Heard Sirens," *The News* (Paterson, NJ), January 23, 1952.
2. Ibid.
3. Geoffrey Gould and Frances Lewine, "Drive to Move Newark Airport After Second Elizabeth Crash," *The News* (Paterson, NJ), January 23, 1952.
4. Ibid.
5. "Sidelights on Airliner Wreck," *The News* (Paterson, NJ), January 23, 1952, via the Associated Press.
6. "Why Umbrella of Death," *The News* (Paterson, NJ), February 11, 1952.
7. Vice, "Why Are We So Obsessed with Plane Crashes?," March 24, 2015, https://www.vice.com/en_us/article/nn9jzk/why-are-we-so-obsessed-with-plane-crashes-186.
8. Burns & McDonnell, "Timeline of Commercial Aviaation," https://www.burnsmcd.com/insightsnews/publications/aviation-special-report/2011/timeline-of-commercial-aviation.
9. Ibid.
10. "It's a Smaller World," *Newsweek* (October 1958): 93–96.
11. Stephanie Watson, "Modern Airplane Technology: 1950–1999," in *Science and Its Times*, vol. 7, *1950 to Present*, edited by Neil Schlager and Josh Lauer (Detroit, MI: Gale, 2001), 506–9, accessed via Gale eBooks, https://link.gale.com/apps/doc/CX3408504649/GVRL?u=kinnehs_ca&sid=GVRL&xid=860f1c13.

12. Henry M. Holden, *Images of Aviation: Newark Airport* (Charleston, SC: Arcadia Publishing, 2009), 7.
13. Clayton Knight, *Plane Crash: The Mysteries of Major Air Disasters and How They Are Solved* (New York: Greenberg Publisher, 1958).
14. Vice, "Why Are We So Obsessed with Plane Crashes?"
15. Ibid.
16. Ibid.
17. Allianz Global Corporate & Specialty, "How Aviation Safety Has Improved," https://www.agcs.allianz.com/news-and-insights/expert-risk-articles/how-aviation-safety-has-improved.html.
18. "Survivors Recall January 1952 Elizabeth Plane Crash," *Union News Daily*, September 26, 2018, https://unionnewsdaily.com/news/elizabeth/40987.
19. "Crash Course: Judy Blume Revisits Her Elizabeth Childhood," *New Jersey Monthly*, June 2, 2015, https://njmonthly.com/articles/jersey-living/crash-course-judy-blume-elizabeth-plane-crashes.

Chapter 1

20. John Cunningham, *New Jersey: A Mirror on America* (Florham Park, NJ: Afton Publishing, 1978), 316.
21. John Cunningham, *Newark* (Newark: New Jersey Historical Society, 1988), 268.
22. Ibid.
23. Holden, *Images of Aviation*.
24. Cunningham, *Newark*, 270.
25. Ibid.
26. Holden, *Images of Aviation*, 7.
27. Cunningham, *Newark*, 270.
28. Ibid.
29. Holden, *Images of Aviation*, 8.
30. Ibid., 9.
31. "Newark Airport Vital for Air Defense," *Central New Jersey Home News* (New Brunswick, NJ), June 3, 1940, 4.
32. "Future of Newark Airport in Doubt," *Paterson (NJ) Morning Call*, May 28, 1940, 26.
33. "Newark Airport Closes as Traffic Goes to N.Y.," *Morning Post* (Camden, NJ), June 1, 1940, 2.

34. "Future of Newark Airport in Doubt," *Paterson Morning Call* (Paterson, NJ), May 28, 1940, 26.
35. Ibid.
36. R.G. Grant, *Flight: The Complete History* (New York: Penguin Random House, 2017), 142.
37. Ibid.
38. Holden, *Images of Aviation*, 62.
39. Ibid., 9.
40. Cunningham, *Newark*, 302.
41. "Newark Airport to Be Larger by Two Thirds: Port Authority of N.Y. to Spend $1,200,000 on Expansion Program," *Herald News* (Passaic, NJ), September 9, 1949, 2.
42. Cunningham, *Newark*, 303.
43. Knight, *Plane Crash*, 199.
44. Ibid.
45. "Newark Airport Plan Endorsers Have Their Day," *The Record* (Hackensack, NJ), October 16, 1947, 2.

Chapter 2

46. Cunningham, *Newark*, 303.
47. "Ellenstein Wars on Noise and Nuisance of Newark Airport," *Paterson (NJ) Evening News*, June 16, 1950, 2.
48. Cunningham, *Newark*, 303.
49. "Reducing Airplane Noise," *The Record* (Hackensack, NJ), June 25, 1948, 28.
50. Cunningham, *Newark*, 303.
51. "Noisy Airplane Complaints Up," *Asbury Park (NJ) Press*, August 7, 1950, 8.
52. "Newark Offers Plan to Tone Down Planes," *Courier News* (Bridgewater, NJ), August 28, 1946, 1.
53. "Ellenstein Wars on Noise and Nuisance of Newark Airport."
54. Ibid.
55. "Newark Airport Plan Endorsers Have Their Day."
56. "Ellenstein Wars on Noise and Nuisance of Newark Airport."
57. "Noisy Airplane Complaints Up."
58. Ibid.
59. Ibid.

60. Ibid.
61. "Sprawling Newark Airport Is Turned into Ghost Field," *Morning Call* (Paterson, NJ), February 12, 1952, 24.
62. "Three Inquires in Probst Crash," *Herald-News* (Passaic, NJ), September 14, 1932, 1.
63. Ibid.
64. "Sprawling Newark Airport Is Turned into Ghost Field."
65. Wolfram Schlenker and W. Reed Walker, "Airports, Air Pollution, and Contemporaneous Health," Review of Economic Studies, July 2015, http://www.restud.com/wp-content/uploads/2015/09/MS17397manuscript.pdf.
66. Knight, *Plane Crash*, 40.
67. Ibid.
68. Ibid., 41.
69. Ibid.
70. Ibid.

Chapter 3

71. "Eyewitness Tell Stories of Tragedy," *Paterson (NJ) Morning Call*, December 17, 1951, 14.
72. Ibid.
73. Ibid.
74. Ibid.
75. Ibid.
76. Ibid.
77. Ibid.
78. Ibid.
79. "Passengers Died Screaming, Trapped in Cut-Rate Plane," *The News* (Paterson, NJ), December 17, 1951, 1.
80. Ibid.
81. Ibid.
82. "Florida-Bound Airliner Afire, Falls at Edge of Midtown Elizabeth," *Morning Call* (Paterson, NJ), December 17, 1951, 1.
83. Ibid.
84. "Elizabeth's Citizens Spur Sift; 56 Dead," *The News* (Paterson, NJ), December 17, 1951, 1.
85. Ibid.

86. Ibid.

87. "Passengers Died Screaming, Trapped in Cut-Rate Plane," 15.

88. Knight, *Plane Crash*, 200.

89. "Passengers Died Screaming, Trapped in Cut-Rate Plane," 15.

90. "Florida-Bound Airliner Afire, Falls at Edge of Midtown Elizabeth," 14.

91. "Passengers Died Screaming, Trapped in Cut-Rate Plane," 15.

92. "Florida-Bound Airliner Afire, Falls at Edge of Midtown Elizabeth," 14.

93. "Passengers Died Screaming, Trapped in Cut-Rate Plane," 15.

94. "Morgue Admits First Relatives," *The News* (Paterson, NJ), December 17, 1951, 15.

95. Ibid.

96. Ibid.

97. Ibid.

98. "Elizabeth's Citizens Spur Sift; 56 Dead," 1.

99. "Airport Surveyed as 'Health Menace,'" *Courier News* (Bridgewater, NJ), December 18, 1951, 1.

100. "Seven Towns Join in Fight Against Newark Airport," *Morning Call* (Paterson, NJ), December 20, 1951, 19.

101. Ibid.

102. "6 Agencies Probe Crash in Elizabeth," *Courier News* (Bridgewater, NJ), December 18, 1951, 1.

103. "Air Probe Told of Engine Fire," *Asbury Park (NJ) Press*, January 12, 1952, 2.

104. "Plane Crash Views Heard," *Courier News* (Bridgewater, NJ), January 11, 1952, 2.

105. Ibid.

106. "Fire Preceded Plane's Crash," *Asbury Park (NJ) Press*, January 13, 1952, 1.

107. Aviation Safety Network, Flight Safety Foundation, "ASN Aircraft accident Curtiss C-46F-1-CU Commando N1678M Newark International Airport, NJ (EWR)," December 16, 1951, https://aviation-safety.net/database/record.php?id=19511216-0.

108. Cunningham, *Newark*, 304.

Chapter 4

109. "Priest Was Blessing Home; Then Plane, Chaos Struck," *The Record* (Hackensack, NJ), January 23, 1952, 4.

110. Ibid.

111. Ibid.

112. Ibid.

113. Ibid.

114. Cunningham, *Newark*, 304.

115. Knight, *Plane Crash*, 200.

116. Ibid., 201.

117. Cunningham, *Newark*, 304.

118. "Beam Goes Over Schools, Big Hospital," *Herald News* (Passaic, NJ), January 23, 1952, 2.

119. Stu Beitler (submitted), "Elizabeth, NJ Plane Crash Kills 28, Jan 1952," GenDisasters, http://www.gendisasters.com/new-jersey/3934/elizabeth%2C-nj-plane-crash-kills-28%2C-jan-1952.

120. Cunningham, *Newark*, 304.

121. "Elizabeth Again Scene of Crash," *The Record* (Hackensack, NJ), January 23, 1952, 1.

122. Beitler, "Elizabeth, NJ Plane Crash Kills 28, Jan 1952."

123. "Firemen Hunt for More Bodies in 3 Houses Airliners Smashed," *Herald News* (Passaic, NJ), January 23, 1952, 1.

124. Ibid.

125. "Heroism and Horror Mark Air Tragedy," *Morning Call* (Paterson, NJ), January 23, 1952, 1.

126. "Bodies Lie in Rain, Mud; Screams Heard in Flames," *Herald News* (Passaic, NJ), January 23, 1952, 1.

127. Ibid.

128. "Don Newcombe Helps at Scene," *The News* (Paterson, NJ), January 23, 1952, 38.

129. "Heroism and Horror Mark Air Tragedy," 2.

130. Ibid.

131. "Bodies Lie in Rain, Mud; Screams Heard in Flames," 2.

132. "Heroism and Horror Mark Air Tragedy," 2.

133. "One Daughter Rushed to Hospital, Second Killed in Air Crash," *The News* (Paterson, NJ), January 23, 1952, 38.

134. "Sidelights on Airliner Wreck," *The News* (Paterson, NJ), January 23, 1952, 38.

135. Ibid.

136. Ibid.

137. Ibid.

138. "Elizabeth Again Scene of Crash," 4.

139. "Patterson Had Remarked on Suddenness of Death," *The Record* (Hackensack, NJ), January 23, 1952, 4.

140. "Patterson Death Mourned by Nation," *The News* (Paterson, NJ), January 23, 1952, 38.

141. Pelletreau, "Pilot Lived Three Blocks from Crash Scene," 38.

142. Ibid.

143. "Grim Evidence of Tragedy in Airliner Debris," *The News* (Paterson, NJ), January 23, 1952, 38.

144. "Ban Sought on Flights Over City," *Central New Jersey Home News* (New Brunswick, NJ), January 25, 1952, 1.

145. Ibid.

146. Ibid.

147. Ibid.

148. Ibid.

149. Ibid.

150. Ibid.

151. "Newark Airport Inquiry Opened," *Central New Jersey Home News* (New Brunswick, NJ), January 28, 1952, 1.

152. Aviation Safety Network, Flight Safety Foundation, "ASN Aircraft accident Convair CV-240-0 N94229 Newark International Airport, NJ (EWR)," January 22, 1952, https://aviation-safety.net/database/record.php?id=19520122-0.

153. "Cause of 2nd Crash at Elizabeth Called Unsolved by CAB," *Courier News* (Bridgewater, NJ), April 28, 1952, 1.

154. Ibid.

Chapter 5

155. "Takeoff OK, Stewardess Tells CAB," *Morning Call* (Paterson, NJ), February 12, 1952.

156. Ibid.

157. Ibid.

158. "Newark Airport Dead, Says Canfield; Death Toll Now 31," *Morning Call* (Paterson, NJ), February 12, 1952, 1.

159. Ibid., 30.

160. Ibid.

161. Ibid.

162. Ibid.

163. Stu Beitler (submitted), "Elizabeth, NJ 34 Killed in Another Air Crash, Feb 1952," GenDisasters, http://www.gendisasters.com/new-jersey/3955/elizabeth-nj-34-killed-in-another-air-crash-feb-1952?page=0,1.

164. "Saw Flaming Torches," *The News* (Paterson, NJ), February 11, 1952, 30.

165. Ibid.

166. "Paterson Rescuers Found Elizabeth's Dazed Residents Seething with Anger," *The News* (Paterson, NJ), February 11, 1952.

167. "Cop Couldn't Leave Dead Child in Burning Apartment House," *Morning Call* (Paterson, NJ), February 12, 1952, 24.

168. Ibid.

169. "Funeral Home Plays Morbid Role for Third Time," *The News* (Paterson, NJ), February 11, 1952, 30.

170. Ibid.

171. Beitler, "Elizabeth, NJ 34 Killed in Another Air Crash."

172. "Order for Airport Closing Came from Driscoll," *The News* (Paterson, NJ), February 11, 30.

173. Ibid.

174. Ibid.

175. "Queens Residents Demand Removal of Two Airports," *Morning Call* (Paterson, NJ), February 12, 2020, 24.

176. Ibid.

177. "Close Newark Airport," *The News* (Paterson, NJ), February 11, 1952, 30.

178. "No Whitewash in Plane Probe, Says Legislative Group," *The News* (Paterson, NJ), February 21, 1952, 18.

179. "Study Safety Plans for Newark Airport," *Central New Jersey Home News* (New Brunswick, NJ), February 13, 3.

180. "No Whitewash in Plane Probe, Says Legislative Group," 18.

181. Ibid.

182. Ibid.

183. Ibid.

184. Aviation Safety Network, Flight Safety Foundation, "ASN Aircraft accident Douglas DC-6 N90891 Newark International Airport, NJ (EWR)," February 11, 1952, https://aviation-safety.net/database/record.php?id=19520211-0.

185. Knight, *Plane Crash*, 202.

Chapter 6

186. "Expert Says New Runways and Traffic Plan Will Minimize Hazards at Large Airports," *The Record* (Hackensack, NJ), February 28, 1952.

187. Knight, *Plane Crash*, 202.

188. "Air Agency Is Surprised by Sawyer," *Central New Jersey Home News* (New Brunswick, NJ), February 26, 1952, 1.

189. Ibid.

190. "Talks Set on Reopening Newark Port to Air Force," *Courier News* (Bridgewater, NJ), March 19, 1952, 37.

191. Ibid.

192. Ibid.

193. "Military Airplanes at Newark Airport," *Central New Jersey Home News* (New Brunswick, NJ), March 27, 1952, 10.

194. "Airlines Need Newark Airport, Rickenbacker Says; Offers Plan," *Central New Jersey Home News* (New Brunswick, NJ), April 16, 1952, 18.

195. Ibid.

196. Ibid.

197. "Rickenbacker Asks Airport to Use Now: Cites New Safety Program," *Courier News* (Bridgewater, NJ), May 16, 1952, 1.

198. Ibid.

199. Ibid.

200. Ibid.

201. "Protests Set on Reopening Newark Airport," *Central New Jersey Home News* (New Brunswick, NJ), May 12, 1952, 1.

202. "Newark Airport Will Re-Open November 1," *Morning Call* (Paterson, NJ), May 12, 1952, 1.

203. "Protests Set on Reopening Newark Airport," 1.

204. "Doolittle Says Newark Airport Is Safe, Recommends Reopening," *Central New Jersey Home News* (New Brunswick, NJ), May 17, 1952, 1.

Chapter 7

205. "Full Operations Start at Airport," *Asbury Park (NJ) Press*, November 15, 1952, 2.

206. Holden, *Images of Aviation*, 10.

207. "Elizabeth Folk Bitter Over Airport Reopening," *Herald-News* (Passaic, NJ), June 13, 1952, 1.

208. "Newark Airport to Reopen Monday Under New Safety Rules, Protests Due," *Courier News* (Bridgewater, NJ), June 13, 1952, 1.

209. Cunningham, *Newark*, 304.

210. "Elizabeth Folk Bitter Over Airport Reopening," 1.

211. Ibid., 2.

212. "Low-Flying Airliner Arouses Elizabeth," *Courier News* (Bridgewater, NJ), June 21, 1952, 1.

213. "Newark Airport Open Again; Awaits Big Airline Business," *Central New Jersey Home News* (New Brunswick, NJ), June 16, 1952, 1.

214. Ibid.

215. "Stelton Flyer Lands First Plane as Newark Airport Is Reopened," *Courier News* (Bridgewater, NJ), November 15, 1952, 1.

216. "Newark Airport Opens, but Traffic's Lighter," *Herald News* (Passaic, NJ), November 15, 1952, 1.

217. "United Air Lines Needs Radio Electric Mechanics," *The Record* (Hackensack, NJ), December 22, 1952, 36.

218. "Newark Airport Reopening," *Herald News* (Passaic, NJ), November 17, 1952, 12.

219. "Series of Elizabeth Air Crashes Started Year Ago," *The News* (Paterson, NJ), December 16, 1952, 4.

220. Cunningham, *Newark*, 305.

221. Aviation Safety Network, Flight Safety Foundation, "ASN Aircraft accident Learjet 25 N51CA Newark International Airport, NJ (EWR)," March 30, 1983, https://aviation-safety.net/database/record.php?id=19830330-1.

222. "Series of Elizabeth Air Crashes Started Year Ago," 4.

223. National Transportation Safety Board, "Aviation Accident Final Report," via Aviation Safety Network, https://reports.aviation-safety.net/2000/20000425-2_DC10_N39081.pdf.

224. Aviation Safety Network, Flight Safety Foundation, "ASN Aircraft accident McDonnell Douglas DC-10-30 N39081 Newark International Airport, NJ (EWR)," April 25, 2000, https://aviation-safety.net/database/record.php?id=20000425-2.

225. Ibid.

NOTES TO PAGES 96–98

Epilogue

226. "Elizabeth Remembers Disasters," *Daily Record* (Morristown, NJ), January 5, 1992, 34.
227. "Survivors Recall January 1952 Elizabeth Plane Crash."
228. Ibid.
229. Ibid.
230. Port Authority of New York and New Jersey, "Aviation History," https://www.panynj.gov/port-authority/en/about/History/aviation-history-history-about.html.
231. NYC Data, "Infrastructure," Baruch College, Zicklin School of Business, https://www.baruch.cuny.edu/nycdata/infrastructure/airport_newark.html.

ABOUT THE AUTHOR

Peter Zablocki is an author and historian living in Denville, New Jersey. His previous books include *Denville Goes to War: Denville's Story of World War I*, *Denville in World War II* and *The Denville 13: Murder, Redemption and Forgiveness in Small-Town New Jersey*. He is also a contributing writer for *Military History Quarterly*, *American History Magazine*, *Military History Magazine*, *History Magazine Quarterly*, *Honest History Magazine*, *Weird NJ* and *Denville Life Magazine*. When not writing, he co-hosts a podcast with his best friend Tom named *History Teachers Talking*, available on all major podcast platforms. Peter also serves as the Denville Historical Society and Museum's vice-president and is one of Denville's town historians.

Visit us at
www.historypress.com